Consumer MATH

AGS

by
Wilmer L. Jones, Ph.D.

D1572695

American Guidance Service, Inc.
4201 Woodland Road
Circle Pines, MN 55014-1796
1-800-328-2560

Life Skills Mathematics

Printed in the United States of America

ISBN 0-7854-0954-8 (Previously ISBN 0-88671-540-7)

Product Number 90862

V036 17 16 15 14 13 12

Contents

Unit 1: Income

Skill Building: Addition and Subtraction of Decimals   5
Lesson 1: Straight-Time Pay   6
Lesson 2: Overtime Pay   8
Lesson 3: Commission   10
Lesson 4: Gross and Net Pay   12

Unit 2: Savings Accounts

Skill Building: Addition and Subtraction of Decimals   14
Skill Building: Rounding Decimals   15
Lesson 1: Deposit and Withdrawal Slips   16
Lesson 2: Simple Interest   19
Lesson 3: Compound Interest   21
Lesson 4: Passbooks   23

Unit 3: Checking Accounts

Skill Building: Dividing a Decimal by a Whole Number   25
Skill Building: Dividing a Decimal by a Decimal   26
Lesson 1: Deposit Slips   28
Lesson 2: Writing Checks, Part 1   30
Lesson 3: Writing Checks, Part 2   32
Lesson 4: Check Stubs   34
Lesson 5: Running Balance, Part 1   36
Lesson 6: Running Balance, Part 2   38
Consumer Checkpoint 1   40

Unit 4: Planning a Budget

Skill Building: Multiplication of Decimals   41
Lesson 1: Parts of a Budget   43
Lesson 2: Preparing a Budget   45
Lesson 3: Comparing Budgets   47

Unit 5: Consumer Credit

Skill Building: Multiplying by 10, 100, and 1,000   49
Skill Building: Decimals to Percents/Percents to Decimals   50
Lesson 1: Credit Cards   51
Lesson 2: Finance Charges   53
Lesson 3: Installment Buying   55
Lesson 4: Short-Term Loans   57

Unit 6: Purchasing a Car

Skill Building: Finding a Percent of a Number   59
Skill Building: Finding Percent One Number Is of Another   60
Lesson 1: Shopping for a New Car   61
Lesson 2: Buying a Used Car   63
Lesson 3: Financing a Car   65
Lesson 4: Auto Insurance   67
Lesson 5: Depreciation   69
Lesson 6: Driving and Maintaining a Car   71
Consumer Checkpoint 2   73

Unit 7: Taxes

Skill Building: Writing Fractions in Lowest Terms   74
Skill Building: Writing Fractions as Percents   75
Lesson 1: Sales Tax   76
Lesson 2: Real Estate Tax   78
Lesson 3: Federal Income Tax, Part 1   80
Lesson 4: Federal Income Tax, Part 2   82

Unit 8: Investments

Skill Building: Addition and Subtraction of Fractions   84
Lesson 1: Certificates of Deposit   86
Lesson 2: Savings Bonds   88
Lesson 3: Buying Stocks   90
Lesson 4: Stock Dividends   92
Consumer Checkpoint 3   94

End-of-Book Test   95

Addition and Subtraction of Decimals

Rules to Remember:

To add and subtract decimals:

➤ Line up the decimal points under each other.

➤ Add zeros where necessary. The addition of zeros after a decimal point does not change the value of the decimal.

➤ Add or subtract as you would with whole numbers.

Examples:

Add: 12.75 + 4.085 + 16

```
  12.750  ◄── Add zero
   4.085
+ 16.000  ◄── Add zeros
  32.835
     ▲  Decimal point under other decimal points
```

Subtract: 275.5 − 98.653

```
  275.500  ◄── Add zeros
 − 98.653
  176.847
     Ⅱ  Decimal point under other decimal points
```

A Add. Check your answers.

1.	2.	3.	4.	5.	6.
6.25	18.3	32.8	102.3	76.27	92.19
14.86	24.7	9.7	98.9	9.85	100.73
+ 9.37	+ 9.8	+ 18.5	+ 24.6	+ 10.28	+ 86.84

B Subtract to find the difference.

7.	8.	9.	10.	11.	12.
17.5	28.6	2.75	1.78	27.62	14.62
− 8.6	− 12.9	− .89	− .95	− 8.61	− 9.38

Some people are paid a salary based on how many hours they work. The *hourly* rate is the amount of money they earn per hour. The *straight-time* pay is the amount of money earned for a pay period at an hourly rate.

Example: Tom works as a kitchen helper at the Crab Shack. He earns $5.25 per hour. Last week he worked 36 hours. What is his straight-time pay for last week?

Straight-time pay	=	Hours worked	x	Hourly rate

$$= \quad 36 \quad x \quad \$5.25$$
$$= \quad \$189.00$$

The straight-time pay is $189.00.

A   Find the straight-time pay.

	Employee	Hours Worked	Hourly Rate	Straight-Time Pay
1.	Karen	36	$5.35	
2.	Gerard	40	7.00	
3.	Katie	32	5.25	
4.	John	40	7.25	
5.	Keith	28	5.15	
6.	Malcolm	36	5.75	
7.	Lisa	26	7.10	
8.	Paul	37	5.80	
9.	Dominic	31	6.75	
10.	Angelo	38	5.90	
11.	Joyce	40	6.20	

B Find the straight-time pay.

12. Cashier
    Earns $4.75 per hour.
    Worked 30 hours last week.

    Straight-time pay = _____

13. Waitress
    Earns $5.10 per hour.
    Worked 32 hours last week.

    Straight-time pay = _____

14. Library aide
    Earns $4.80 per hour.
    Worked $24\frac{1}{2}$ hours last week.

    Straight-time pay = _____

15. Fast-food attendant
    Earns $5.05 per hour.
    Worked $16\frac{1}{2}$ hours last week.

    Straight-time pay = _____

16. Steve plays for a local band. He earns $8.50 per hour.

    Last week he worked $4\frac{1}{2}$ hours on Friday and 5 hours on Saturday.

    How much did he earn? _____

17. Christa has a part-time job at Tasty Burgers.

    She is paid at an hourly rate of $4.25 an hour.

    How much did she earn last week if she worked 40 hours? _____

18. Horace earns $11.25 as a construction worker. Last week he worked these hours:

Monday	Tuesday	Wednesday	Thursday	Friday
8	8	6	8	6

    What was Horace's straight-time pay for the week? _____

    Part-Time Help.
    Smith's Deli
    Earnings—$4.60/hr.

    ---

19. What is Tyrone's straight-time pay if he works 20 hours per week at Smith's Deli?

    _____

20. How much can Katherine earn each week if she works $18\frac{1}{2}$ hours at Smith's Deli?

    _____

Overtime Pay

Some employees are paid at a regular rate for the first 40 hours they work each week. If they work more than 8 hours in one day or more than 40 hours in one week, they are paid at an *overtime rate*. The overtime rate is normally 1.5 times the regular hourly rate.

The *gross pay* is the sum of the straight-time pay and the overtime pay.

Example: Christa works as a fast-food attendant for Tasty Burgers. Last week she worked 46 hours. If her regular rate is $4.80 an hour, what is her gross pay for the week?

Straight-time pay	=	Hours worked	x	Hourly rate

= 40   x $4.80
= $192.00

Overtime pay	=	Hours worked	x	Hourly rate	x	Overtime rate

= 6   x $4.80   x   1.5
= $43.20

Gross pay	=	Straight-time pay	+	Overtime pay

= $192.00   + $43.20
= $235.20

Christa's gross pay is $235.20.

ger	.79
r	69
eseburger	1 29
;	75
	.65

Cheeseburger	79
Hamburger	.69
Double Cheeseburger	1 29
Large Fries	.75
Small Fries	.65

A Find the gross pay. The overtime rate is 1.5 times the regular hourly rate.

	Regular Hours	Straight-Time Rate	Straight-Time Pay	Overtime Hours	Overtime Pay	Gross Pay
1.	40	$4.60		4		
2.	40	5.00		8		
3.	40	4.84		10		
4.	36	6.00		6		
5.	40	5.10		12		
6.	36	4.90		2		
7.	40	6.70		4		
8.	40	8.12		10		
9.	38	7.25		6		

B Find the gross pay. All hours over 40 are paid at the time-and-a-half rate. The regular rate is $7.20.

10. 42 hours _____   **11.** 60 hours _____   **12.** $48\frac{1}{2}$ hours _____

13. 38 hours _____   **14.** $24\frac{1}{2}$ hours _____   **15.** 46 hours _____

16. 45 hours _____   **17.** 44 hours _____   **18.** 41 hours _____

19. Dental assistant
Regular hourly rate: $9.20
Worked 48 hours.

Gross pay = _____

20. Electronic technician
Regular hourly rate: $10.50
Worked 42 hours.

Gross pay = _____

 Sam is a cable TV installer. His regular hourly rate is $9.15. He is paid time and a half for overtime. What is his gross pay for a week in which he worked 36 regular hours and 6 overtime hours?
_____

Some salespeople are paid an additional amount of money for the sales that they complete. This payment is called a *commission*. The commission is a percent of total sales.

Example: Indira works at a computer store. She earns $5.50 per hour plus a 7% commission on all computer equipment she sells. On Tuesday, she worked 8 hours and sold a $3,000 computer. What were Indira's gross earnings on Tuesday?

| Straight-time pay | = | Hours worked | x | Hourly rate |

$$= \quad 8 \qquad \qquad x \qquad \quad \$5.50$$
$$= \quad \$44.00$$

| Commission | = | Total sales | x | Percent of commission |

$$= \quad \$3,000 \qquad x \qquad .07$$
$$= \quad \$210.00$$

| Gross pay | = | Straight-time pay | + | Commission |

$$= \quad \$\ 44.00 \qquad \qquad + \qquad \$210.00$$
$$= \quad \$254.00$$

Indira's gross earnings were $254.

A Find the commission and gross pay.

	Hourly Rate	Hours Worked	Total Sales	Rate of Commission	Commission	Gross Pay
1.	$4.35	6	$86	6%		
2.	$5.25	40	$3,800	3%		
3.	$7.50	15	$400	20%		
4.	$6.75	20	$9,550	30%		
5.	$7.00	36	$7,200	15%		
6.	$5.50	36	$12,300	4%		
7.	$6.70	40	$8,800	5%		
8.	$8.12	40	$4,200	6%		
9.	$7.25	38	$1,900	12%		
10.	$5.45	34	$4,400	5%		

B Find the gross pay.

11. $4.35 per hour; 4 hours; $86 in sales; 6% commission _____

12. $5.25 per hour; 40 hours; $380 in sales; 3% commission _____

13. $4.50 per hour; 20 hours; $300 in sales; 5% commission _____

C Find the commission.

14. $49,660 in sales; $6\frac{1}{2}$% commission _____

15. $210,000 in sales; 4% commission _____

16. $65,400 in sales; 5% commission _____

17. Mr. Vilan, a realtor, sold a house for $156,000.

He earned a 7% commission on the first $100,000 and 3% on the amount over $100,000.

How much did Mr. Vilan earn? _____

18. Paula works at Trendy Fashions. Last weekend she sold $1,420 in merchandise.

In addition to her hourly wage, she earns a 4% commission on all sales.

How much commission did Paula earn? _____

19. JoAnn Williams is an insurance agent.

She earns a 6% commission on each policy she writes.

How much commission will she earn if she writes a policy for $160,000? _____

20. Ted worked 25 hours last week and earned $630.

30% of his salary was commission.

How much did Ted earn in commission? _____

Jon and Lia work at the Auto Emporium. Jon is paid a straight-time salary of $11.40 per hour. Lia earns $4.60 per hour and a 2% commission on all sales she makes. Last week, both Jon and Lia worked 40 hours and each sold a car for $18,900. Who earned more money? How much more?

_____

U N I T 1

The amount of money earned by a worker is called his or her *gross pay*. *Deductions* are the amount subtracted from a worker's pay. They include items such as taxes, insurance, and union dues. The *net pay*, or *take-home pay*, is the amount received after the deductions are subtracted.

Example: Sharon earns \$4.60 an hour. She worked 36 hours last week. Her deductions were \$34.00. What is her net pay?

Gross pay	=	Hours worked	x	Hourly rate

              =   36   x   \$4.60

              =   \$165.60

Net pay	=	Gross pay	–	Deductions

              =   \$165.60   –   \$34.00

              =   \$131.60

Sharon's net pay is \$131.60.

A Find the net pay.

1. Gross pay: \$176.50
   Deductions:
       Fed. withholding tax: \$22.75
       F.I.C.A.: \$12.32

   _____

2. Gross pay: \$325.40
   Deductions:
       Fed. withholding tax: \$60.25
       F.I.C.A.: \$21.95

   _____

3. Gross pay: \$550.00
   Deductions:
       Fed. withholding tax: \$45.50
       F.I.C.A.: \$45.60
       State Tax: \$16.00

   _____

4. Gross pay: \$326.50
   Deductions:
       Fed. withholding tax: \$59.67
       F.I.C.A.: \$26.25
       Insurance: \$8.10

   _____

B Complete the table for each worker.

Name	Hours Worked	Rate per Hour	Gross Pay	Deductions	Net Pay
5. Alex	40	$7.75		$82.40	
6. Megan	36	5.00		38.16	
7. Chris	28	6.35		30.12	
8. Charvon	32	5.12		42.75	
9. Andrew	40	4.45		50.63	
10. Richard	35	5.80		57.72	
11. Jennifer	$24\frac{1}{2}$	8.60		78.40	
12. Heather	30	6.75		46.45	
13. Tonya	37	4.80		53.80	
14. Carlos	40	6.55		61.92	
15. Roberta	38	5.90		54.71	
16. LeRoy	39	7.10		62.43	

17. A steelworker earns $22.50 per hour and works 36 hours per week. His deductions are $168.95. What is his net pay? _____

18. A carpenter works a 48-hour week. She is paid time and a half for all hours over 40. Her hourly rate is $16.00 per hour. Her deductions are $180.00. Find her net pay. _____

C Find the net pay.

19.

Department	Employee	Check#	Gross Pay	Net Pay	
27	Scott Jones	2745	$122.50		
DEDUCTIONS					
FED. W.T.	F.I.C.A.	State	Insurance	Union Dues	Others
$12.15	$8.72	$4.26	$3.75	——	——

20.

Department	Employee	Check#	Gross Pay	Net Pay	
18	Jan Baire	4321	$540.00		
DEDUCTIONS					
FED. W.T.	F.I.C.A.	State	Insurance	Union Dues	Others
$70.25	$37.05	——	$19.25	$10.50	$18.00

Addition and Subtraction of Decimals

A Add. Check your answers.

1.	2.	3.	4.	5.	6.
7.62	18.3	276.4	62.53	1.762	12.75
4.95	45.7	19.8	8.76	9.468	318.40
6.08	16.4	42.7	14.12	3.075	92.75
+ 4.73	+ 13.9	+ 117.4	+ 95.08	+ 8.108	+ 117.16

7. 27.3 + 4.98 + 7.23 = _____

8. 193.6 + 72.84 + 9.6 = _____

9. 4.723 + 6.2 + 13.25 = _____

10. 12 + 7.5 + 8.62 = _____

B Subtract. Check your answers.

11.	12.	13.
273.4	18.25	126.3
– 19.6	– 14.19	– 78.6

14.	15.	16.
27.65	103.65	1,078.1
– 18.27	– 94.23	– 938.2

17. 17.6 – 4.8 = _____

18. 28.2 – 17.9 = _____

19. 100.6 – 78.3 = _____

20. 15.95 – 9.26 = _____

21. 14.68 – 10.72 = _____

22. 375.6 – 273.4 = _____

23. 12 – 9.35 = _____

24. 36 – 31.26 = _____

25. 400 – 372.82 = _____

26. 226 – 28.4 = _____

 John purchased 4 tires for his car at $275.62, new shock absorbers for $69.65, and 8 spark plugs for $9.95. What was his total bill?

_____

Rounding Decimals

Rules to Remember:

To round decimals, look to the right of the place to which you are rounding.

➤ If the digit is 5 or more, round up.

➤ If the digit is 4 or less, round down.

Examples:

Round 2.764 to the nearest whole number.

2.764

Digit to the right is 5 or more. Round up.

2.764 rounded to the nearest whole number is 3.

Round 3.273 to the nearest hundredth.

3.273

Digit to the right is 4 or less. Round down.

3.273 rounded to the nearest hundredth is 3.27.

A Round to the nearest whole number.

1. 7.2 _____

2. 18.6 _____

3. 29.34 _____

4. 8.07 _____

B Round to the nearest tenth.

5. .78 _____

6. 4.52 _____

7. .063 _____

8. 12.637 _____

C Round to the nearest hundredth.

9. .723 _____

10. 4.686 _____

11. .0764 _____

12. 24.004 _____

13. .0988 _____

14. 15.676 _____

15. The unit cost of pencils purchased by the city's public schools is
    $.0435 each. Round to the nearest cent.

_____

Deposit and Withdrawal Slips

People save money for many reasons. One of the ways to save is to open a savings account at a bank, credit union, or savings and loan association.

To open a savings account, a *deposit* is made. *Deposit slips* are used for making deposits.

Example: Jeff Baire has a savings account at the Calvert Springs Savings and Loan Association. Each month he makes a $100 deposit.

Check Deposit

Cash Deposit

Account Number

DEPOSIT
ACCOUNT NO. *27-402-873*

DATE *April 12* 19 *96*

Name *Jeff Baire*

SIGNATURE REQUIRED FOR CASH BACK

Calvert Springs SAVINGS AND LOAN ASSOCIATION

FUNDS MAY NOT BE AVAILABLE FOR IMMEDIATE WITHDRAWAL. CHECKS AND OTHER ITEMS ARE RECEIVED FOR DEPOSIT SUBJECT TO THE PROVISIONS OF THE UNIFORM COMMERICAL CODE.

CASH	CURRENCY	43.00	
	COIN		
LIST CHECKS SINGLY		57.00	
TOTAL FROM OTHER SIDE			
TOTAL		100.00	
LESS CASH RECEIVED		0	
NET DEPOSIT		100.00	

Total Deposit

A Find the total deposit.

1. Steven Cox
    Deposits:
    Check: $12.75
    Cash: $42.95

    Total deposit? _____

2. Marilou Evans
    Deposits:
    Check: $72.50
    Cash: $125.00

    Total deposit? _____

3. Bob Klohr
    Deposits:
    Check: $96.15
    Cash: $152.90

    Total deposit? _____

4. Maggie Church
    Deposits:
    Check: $89.76
    Cash: $34.32

    Total deposit? _____

5. Rich Petersen
    Deposits:
    Checks: $138.90, $112.11
    Cash: $175.00

    Total deposit? _____

6. Keesha Burk
    Deposits:
    Checks: $123.45, $7.43
    Cash: $82.50

    Total deposit? _____

B Complete the deposit slip.

7. Bill Gerardi; deposits of $125.00 cash and checks of $48.90 and $116.28 on May 20, 1997, in his account 51-3829-70

DEPOSIT

ACCOUNT NO. _____

DATE _____ 19 _____

Name _____

_____

SIGNATURE REQUIRED FOR CASH BACK

Calvert Springs SAVINGS AND LOAN ASSOCIATION

FUNDS MAY NOT BE AVAILABLE FOR IMMEDIATE WITHDRAWAL. CHECKS AND OTHER ITEMS ARE RECEIVED FOR DEPOSIT SUBJECT TO THE PROVISIONS OF THE UNIFORM COMMERICAL CODE.

	CURRENCY		
CASH			
	COIN		
LIST CHECKS SINGLY			
TOTAL FROM OTHER SIDE			
TOTAL			
LESS CASH RECEIVED			
NET DEPOSIT			

‖ ■ 0 0333 2 ‖ ■   ■ ■ 0 5 2 0 0 0 6 1 8 ‖ ■

When you wish to take money out of your account, a *withdrawal slip* is used.

Account Number

SAVINGS WITHDRAWAL

DATE ____ March 30 ____ 19 _96_

NAME _Jeff Baire_

ACCOUNT NO. _____ 27-402-873 _____

Fifty and no/100 ——————————————— DOLLARS $ | 50 | 00 |

DEDUCT ABOVE SUM FROM MY SAVINGS ACCOUNT ON DEPOSIT

SIGN HERE _Jeff Baire_ ◀———————————————

Amount to be Withdrawn

Signature

Calvert Springs SAVINGS AND LOAN ASSOCIATION

‖ ■ 0 0333 2 ‖ ■   ■ ■ 0 5 2 0 0 0 6 1 8 ‖ ■

C Complete the withdrawal slips.

8. Steven Haar; withdrawal of $125.00 on June 15, 1998; account number 175–08–612

SAVINGS WITHDRAWAL   DATE _____ 19 _____

NAME _____ ACCOUNT NO. _____

_____ DOLLARS **$** [|]

DEDUCT ABOVE SUM FROM MY SAVINGS ACCOUNT ON DEPOSIT

SIGN HERE _____

Calvert Springs SAVINGS AND LOAN ASSOCIATION

‖■ 0 0333 2 ‖ ■ ■■ 0 5 2 0 0 0 6 1 8 ‖ ■

9. Ann Kasper; withdrawal of $245.00 on May 29, 1999; account number 314–30–697

SAVINGS WITHDRAWAL   DATE _____ 19 _____

NAME _____ ACCOUNT NO. _____

_____ DOLLARS **$** [|]

DEDUCT ABOVE SUM FROM MY SAVINGS ACCOUNT ON DEPOSIT

SIGN HERE _____

Calvert Springs SAVINGS AND LOAN ASSOCIATION

‖■ 0 0333 2 ‖ ■ ■■ 0 5 2 0 0 0 6 1 8 ‖ ■

Simple Interest

When money is deposited in a savings account, it earns *interest*. Interest is paid to you for the use of your money. The bank lends money to someone else and charges them for its use. The *principal* is the amount of money earning interest. The *annual interest rate* is the percent of the principal that is earned in one year. The *time* the principal is used is always expressed in terms of a year. *Simple interest* is interest paid only on the original principal.

Example: Christa Jones has $450.00 deposited in a savings account with an annual interest rate of 6%. After 6 months she wanted to find out how much interest she had earned.

Interest = Principal x Rate x Time

$$= \$450 \times .06 \times \frac{1}{2} \longleftarrow \text{ 6 months} = \frac{1}{2} \text{ year}$$

$$= \$450 \times .03 \longleftarrow$$

$\frac{1}{2} \times .06 = .03$

$$= \$13.50$$

The interest earned in 6 months was $13.50.

A Find the interest on these accounts for one year.

Principal	Rate	Interest
1. $200	5%	_____
2. $1,200	6%	_____
3. $650	4%	_____
4. $2,000	$5\frac{1}{2}$%	_____
5. $4,000	8%	_____
6. $3,000	7%	_____
7. $750	5%	_____
8. $3,400	4%	_____

Principal	Rate	Interest
9. $800	$6\frac{1}{2}$%	_____
10. $2,400	7%	_____
11. $900	$6\frac{1}{4}$%	_____
12. $2,500	6.4%	_____
13. $6,000	7.5%	_____
14. $2,600	5.5%	_____
15. $1,900	6.2%	_____
16. $830	4.5%	_____

B Find the interest.

17. John Stone

    $600 on deposit

    7% annual interest rate

    Time: 6 months

    _____

18. Elena Dominguez

    $1,500 on deposit

    6% annual interest rate

    Time: 3 months

    _____

19. Lynn Fong

    $2,400 on deposit

    5% annual interest rate

    Time: 9 months

    _____

20. James Robinson

    $3,000 on deposit

    6% annual interest rate

    Time: $1\frac{1}{2}$ years

    _____

Person	Principal	Annual Rate	Time	Interest
21. Gary Sanford	$650	$5\frac{1}{2}$%	1 yr.	
22. Sharon Stanic	7,000	7%	2 yr.	
23. Tyrone Willis	495	6%	6 months	
24. Juan Vilan	1,550	8%	9 months	
25. Fred Kessler	400	6.9%	1 yr.	
26. Tina Nguyen	4,500	6%	15 months	
27. Karen Ramos	2,750	$5\frac{1}{2}$%	6 months	
28. Keith Kolbe	900	$4\frac{1}{2}$%	1 yr.	
29. Sharron Reid	3,680	7.5%	2 yr.	
30. Chris Lightfoot	765	8%	9 months	

Terri had $1,200 deposited in a savings account paying an annual interest rate of 6%. Find the simple interest for two years.

_____

Compound Interest

Interest earned on a savings account is added to the account. The new balance is used as the principal for the next interest period. *Compound interest* is interest earned on the original principal as well as all the interest earned during previous interest periods.

Example: Dick Heilman has $1,000 deposited in a savings account with an annual interest rate of 8%. The interest on the account compounds quarterly. What is the amount in his account after 6 months?

Interest   = Principal x Rate x Time
         = $1,000 x .08 x $\frac{1}{4}$ ◄──────── **First quarter = 3 months**
                                = $1,000 x .02
         = $20.00

For the first quarter, the new principal is $1,000 + $20.00 interest, or $1,020.

Interest   = Principal x Rate x Time
         = $1,020 x .08 x $\frac{1}{4}$ ◄──────── **Second quarter = 3 months**
                                = $20.40

For the second quarter, the new principal is $1,020 + $20.40, or $1,040.40. The amount after 6 months is $1,040.40.

A Find the interest for the third and fourth quarters.

1. How much interest is earned in the third quarter of Mr. Heilman's account? _____

2. What is the balance of his account after the third quarter? _____

3. How much interest is earned in the fourth quarter of Mr. Heilman's account? _____

4. What is the balance of his account after the fourth quarter? _____

B Find the interest for the first two quarters for each principal below.

	5.	6.	7.	8.
Principal	$500	$2,000	$4,000	$2,400
Annual Interest Rate	4%	8%	6%	8%
First Principal Interest				
Amount				
Second Principal Interest				
Amount				

C Find the balance of each account.

9. Margaret Klohr

   Principal: $700

   6% annual interest

   rate compounded quarterly

   What is the amount in the

   account after 2 quarters?

   _____

10. James Causey

    Principal: $1,000

    5% annual interest rate

    compounded semiannually

    (every 6 months)

    What is the amount in the

    account after 1 year?

    _____

11. Katie Wilson

    Principal: $2,500

    4% annual interest

    rate compounded semiannually

    What is the amount in the

    account after 2 years?

    _____

12. Paul Arroyo

    Principal: $1,200

    7% annual interest rate

    compounded quarterly

    What is the amount in the

    account after 3 quarters?

    _____

13. Jerri Chung

    Principal: $1,800

    $5\frac{1}{2}$% annual interest

    rate compounded quarterly

    What is the amount in the

    account after 1 quarter?

    _____

14. Tom Blake

    Principal: $750

    10% annual interest rate

    compounded semiannually

    What is the amount in the

    account after 6 months?

    _____

Tyrone has $4,000 deposited with an annual interest rate of 8%, compounded quarterly. What is the amount in his account after one year?

_____

Passbooks

When you open a savings account, the bank may issue you a *passbook*. When you make a deposit or a withdrawal, a bank teller records the transaction in the passbook. At appropriate times, interest is also entered.

Example: Amanda Lewis has a savings account. On May 5, she deposited $50. The bank teller recorded the deposit and interest for the last quarter. What is the new balance in the passbook?

Amanda Lewis				
Date	**Interest**	**Deposit**	**Withdrawal**	**Balance**
01/27		$25.00		$175.00
03/24		50.00		225.00
04/08		25.00		250.00
05/05	4.10	50.00		304.10

Interest   Deposit   New Balance

A Find the new balance.

	1.	2.	3.	4.	5.
Previous Balance	$475.20	$628.15	$995.12	$1,275.20	$495.22
Interest	12.85	—	60.75	—	18.15
Deposits	45.25	60.95	125.00	250.00	180.00
Withdrawals	—	75.00	—	127.85	115.00
New Balance					

6. On June 3, Joan made a deposit of $120.00 to her savings account. What is the new balance?

Date	**Interest**	**Deposit**	**Withdrawal**	**Balance**
04/21		$25.00		$875.15
06/03		120.00		**6.**

7. David withdrew $75.00 on April 4. The teller also credited $15.25 in interest to his account. What is the new balance in his account?

Date	Interest	Deposit	Withdrawal	Balance
03/03		$50.00		$1,215.28
03/05		$60.00		$1,275.28
04/04	$15.25		$75.00	7.

B Find the balance for each date in this savings account.

Date	Interest	Deposit	Withdrawal	Balance
03/02		$75.00		$628.50
03/16		$50.00		8.
04/01	$12.50			9.
04/07		$75.00		10.
04/21		$90.00		11.
05/03			$85.00	12.
05/27		$120.00		13.
06/20			$95.00	14.
07/01	$14.50	$65.00		15.

Dividing a Decimal by a Whole Number

Rules to Remember:

To divide a decimal by a whole number:

➤ Place the decimal point in the answer above the point in the dividend (number being divided).

➤ Divide as with a whole number.

➤ Sometimes it is necessary to place zeros in the answer.

Examples:

Divide: 9.12 ÷ 24

```
       .38
   24)9.12
     72
     192
     192
       0
```

Divide: 4.717 ÷ 89

```
        .053
   89)4.717
      445
      267
      267
        0
```

Divide. Check your answers.

1. 7)88.2

2. 6)1.836

3. 15).795

4. 2)327.48

5. 9)177.3

6. 6)2.616

7. 6)714.84

8. 12)22.32

9. 16)757.44

10. 72)40.32

11. 9).288

12. 31).1085

Dividing a Decimal by a Decimal

Skill Building

Rules to Remember:

To divide a decimal by a decimal:

➤ Multiply both the divisor and dividend by 10, 100, or 1,000 to make a whole-number divisor.

➤ Place the decimal point in the answer above the decimal point in the dividend after it has been moved.

➤ Divide as with whole numbers.

Examples:

Divide: 8.96 ÷ .32

The divisor is .32 (32 hundredths). Multiply the divisor and the dividend by 100.

$$.32\overline{)8.96}$$

Move the decimal point two places to the right.

$$
\begin{array}{r}
28 \\
32\overline{)896} \\
\underline{64} \\
256 \\
\underline{256} \\
0
\end{array}
$$

Divide: 3.6 ÷ .045

The divisor is .045 (45 thousandths). Multiply the divisor and the dividend by 1,000.

$$.045\overline{)3.600}$$

Move the decimal point three places to the right. Add two zeros.

$$
\begin{array}{r}
80 \\
45\overline{)3600} \\
\underline{360} \\
00
\end{array}
$$

26 UNIT 3 *CHECKING ACCOUNTS*

Divide. Check your answers.

1. $.6\overline{)21.27}$　　　　2. $.08\overline{)1.912}$　　　　3. $.3\overline{).894}$　　　　4. $.05\overline{)1.810}$

5. $.7\overline{).1113}$　　　　6. $.008\overline{).256}$　　　　7. $.9\overline{)228.6}$　　　　8. $.007\overline{)2.989}$

9. $2.3\overline{)8.97}$　　　　10. $.29\overline{).464}$　　　　11. $7.5\overline{)4.50}$　　　　12. $.52\overline{).884}$

13. $.21\overline{)11.97}$　　　　14. $.084\overline{).3024}$　　　　15. $3.7\overline{)236.8}$　　　　16. $8.1\overline{)42.12}$

17. $3.76 \div .4 = $ ＿＿＿＿＿　　　　18. $28 \div .7 = $ ＿＿＿＿＿

19. $2.615 \div .5 = $ ＿＿＿＿＿　　　　20. $65.7 \div .9 = $ ＿＿＿＿＿

21. $.238 \div .7 = $ ＿＿＿＿＿　　　　22. $.1224 \div .8 = $ ＿＿＿＿＿

23. $2.4 \div 1.2 = $ ＿＿＿＿＿　　　　24. $106.6 \div .26 = $ ＿＿＿＿＿

25. $6.643 \div 7.3 = $ ＿＿＿＿＿　　　　26. $104.88 \div .23 = $ ＿＿＿＿＿

27. $9.482 \div 1.1 = $ ＿＿＿＿＿　　　　28. $57. \div .016 = $ ＿＿＿＿＿

A car travels 348 miles and uses 14.5 gallons of gasoline. How far can the car travel on one gallon of gas? ＿＿＿＿＿

Deposit Slips

Checks are often used in place of cash. Paying bills with a check is safer and more convenient than carrying around large amounts of money. To be able to write a check, you must first deposit money into a checking account. Deposit slips are used to record the amount of money deposited.

Example: Scott wishes to deposit two checks, one for $59.95 and the other for $45.00. He also has $40.00 in cash to deposit. This is how the deposit slip was completed:

SCOTT L. JONES			
18 EDGE LANE			
FULTON, NY 13069			

CASH	CURRENCY	40	00
	COIN		
LIST CHECKS SINGLY			
7-19		59	95
7-21		45	00
TOTAL FROM OTHER SIDE			
TOTAL		144	95
LESS CASH RECEIVED			
NET DEPOSIT		144	95

7-89 / 520

◄ List Checks

DATE _____ April 12 _____ 19 96 _____

SIGNATURE REQUIRED FOR CASH BACK

Calvert Springs SAVINGS AND LOAN ASSOCIATION

‖■ 0 0333 2 ‖■ ■■ 0 5 2 0 0 0 6 1 8 ■

6 2 6 59 3 6 ‖ ■

Total Amount Deposited

CHECKS AND OTHER ITEMS ARE RECEIVED FOR DEPOSIT SUBJECT TO THE PROVISIONS OF THE UNIFORM COMMERICAL CODE OR ANY APPLICABLE COLLECTION AGREEMENT.

Scott's Account Number

A Fill in the deposit slip and find the total deposit.

1. Deposit slip for Mary Lee
Check for $162.45
Cash for $62.50

_____

CASH	CURRENCY		
	COIN		
LIST CHECKS SINGLY			
TOTAL FROM OTHER SIDE			
TOTAL			
LESS CASH RECEIVED			
NET DEPOSIT			

2. Deposit slip for Jim Ott
Checks for $92.50 and $117.25
Cash for $118.40

_____

CASH	CURRENCY		
	COIN		
LIST CHECKS SINGLY			
TOTAL FROM OTHER SIDE			
TOTAL			
LESS CASH RECEIVED			
NET DEPOSIT			

B Fill in each deposit slip and find the total deposit.

3. Checks for $12.95 and $27.60
$75.00 in cash

CASH	CURRENCY	
	COIN	
LIST CHECKS SINGLY		
TOTAL FROM OTHER SIDE		
TOTAL		
LESS CASH RECEIVED		
NET DEPOSIT		

4. Checks for $175.90 and $98.75
$120.00 in cash

CASH	CURRENCY	
	COIN	
LIST CHECKS SINGLY		
TOTAL FROM OTHER SIDE		
TOTAL		
LESS CASH RECEIVED		
NET DEPOSIT		

5. Checks for $92.68, $171.75, and $28.40
$125.00 in cash

CASH	CURRENCY	
	COIN	
LIST CHECKS SINGLY		
TOTAL FROM OTHER SIDE		
TOTAL		
LESS CASH RECEIVED		
NET DEPOSIT		

6. Checks for $250, $198.50, and $217.85
$215.80 in cash

CASH	CURRENCY	
	COIN	
LIST CHECKS SINGLY		
TOTAL FROM OTHER SIDE		
TOTAL		
LESS CASH RECEIVED		
NET DEPOSIT		

7. Checks for $45.90 and $72.85
$85.00 in cash

CASH	CURRENCY	
	COIN	
LIST CHECKS SINGLY		
TOTAL FROM OTHER SIDE		
TOTAL		
LESS CASH RECEIVED		
NET DEPOSIT		

8. Checks for $285.00, $98.25, and $162.50
$105.75 in cash

CASH	CURRENCY	
	COIN	
LIST CHECKS SINGLY		
TOTAL FROM OTHER SIDE		
TOTAL		
LESS CASH RECEIVED		
NET DEPOSIT		

Tom Foster deposited the following in his checking account: 40 quarters, 40 dimes, 200 one-dollar bills, and a check for $87.55. Find his total deposit. _____

Writing Checks, Part 1

U N I T 3

After a checking account is opened and a deposit made, checks can be written. When the person (payee) receives the check, it is sent to the bank for payment. The bank subtracts the amount of the check from the account of the person writing the check (payer). This is what a completed check looks like:

Example:

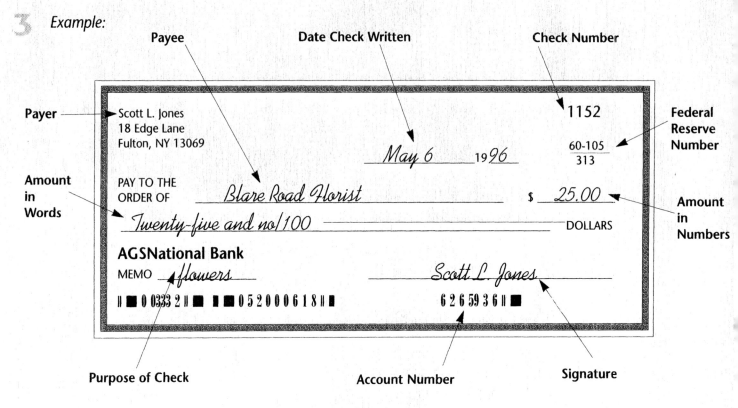

Payee — **Date Check Written** — **Check Number**

Payer — Scott L. Jones / 18 Edge Lane / Fulton, NY 13069 — 1152 — **Federal Reserve Number** — 60-105 / 313

Amount in Words — PAY TO THE ORDER OF *Blare Road Florist* $ *25.00* — **Amount in Numbers**

Twenty-five and no/100 DOLLARS

AGSNational Bank

MEMO *Flowers* — *Scott L. Jones*

⑃◼0 0333 2⑃◼ ⑃◼0 5 2 0 0 0 6 1 8⑃◼ — 6 2 6 59 3 6⑃◼

Purpose of Check — **Account Number** — **Signature**

Things to Remember:

➤ Write the date the check is written. Do not date ahead.

➤ Always fill in the payee's name. Never leave it blank.

➤ Start at the left when writing the amount in numbers. Do not leave space after the dollar sign.

➤ Write the amount in words carefully. Fill the incomplete space with a line.

➤ Sign the check, but never sign before filling in all the blanks.

Write each amount in words as it would appear on a check.

1. $20.75 _____ DOLLARS

2. $125.00 _____ DOLLARS

3. $438.92 _____ DOLLARS

4. $1,475.00 _____ DOLLARS

5. $24,200 _____ DOLLARS

JOHN BROWN   197
26 MAPLE AVE.
GARY, IN 46401   60-105
                          _March 6_____ 19 _96_   ‾‾‾‾‾
                                                                    313

PAY TO THE
ORDER OF   _Jim's Auto Clinic_____ $ _45.00_

_Forty-five and no/100_____ DOLLARS

AGSNational Bank

MEMO _tune-up and oil change_____   _John Brown_____

‖ ■ 0 0333 2 ‖ ■   ■ ■ 0 5 2 0 0 0 6 1 8 ‖ ■

6. Who is the payee? _____

7. What is the amount? _____

8. For what purpose was the check written? _____

KAREN MEUSHAW   48
94 OAK PLACE
ATLANTA, GA 30304   60-105
                          _August 5_____ 19 _96_   ‾‾‾‾‾
                                                                    313
PAY TO THE
ORDER OF   _White Marsh Dental Clinic_____ $ _125.00_

_One hundred twenty-five and no/100_____ DOLLARS

AGSNational Bank

MEMO _dental work_____   _Karen Meushaw_____

‖ ■ 0 0333 2 ‖ ■   ■ ■ 0 5 2 0 0 0 6 1 8 ‖ ■

9. To whose account will the check be charged? _____

10. Was the amount in words written correctly? _____

UNIT 3

To write a check, you do the following:

1. Write the date.

2. Write the name of the person or business to whom the payment is to be made (payee).

3. Write the amount of the check in numerals.

4. Write the amount of the check in words.

5. Write a note on the check to show its purpose.

6. Sign the check (payer).

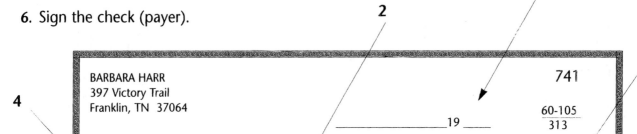

Use the information above each check to complete it.

1.

Date	Payee	Amt. of check	For	Payer
4/21/98	Mary's Beauty Shop	$25.00	Haircut	Margaret Allen

MARGARET ALLEN
1261 West Avenue
Chicago, IL 60601

741

60-105
313

_____ 19 _____

PAY TO THE
ORDER OF _____ $ _____

_____ DOLLARS

AGSNational Bank

MEMO _____

⑈■ 0 0333 2 ⑈■ ■■ 0 5 2 0 0 0 6 1 8 ⑈■

2.

Date	Payee	Amt. of check	For	Payer
5/12/96	A-1 Repair Service	$85.75	VCR Repair	Terri Smith

TERRI SMITH   37
7274 Wilson Blvd., Apt. 40
Las Vegas, NV 89115

_____ 19 ____ $\frac{60\text{-}105}{313}$

PAY TO THE
ORDER OF _____ $ _____

_____ DOLLARS

AGS National Bank

MEMO _____   _____

⑈■0 0333 2 ⑈■ ■■0 5 2 0 0 0 6 1 8 ⑈■

3.

Date	Payee	Amt. of check	For	Payer
9/26/96	Allied Auto Service	$137.50	Auto Repair	John Savarese

John Savarese   502
17 Brentwood Drive
Bangor, ME 04401

_____ 19 ____ $\frac{60\text{-}105}{313}$

PAY TO THE
ORDER OF _____ $ _____

_____ DOLLARS

AGS National Bank

MEMO _____   _____

⑈■0 0333 2 ⑈■ ■■0 5 2 0 0 0 6 1 8 ⑈■

4.

Date	Payee	Amt. of check	For	Payer
12/18/96	Giant Foods	$64.75	Food	Kristie Dando

Kristie Dando   164
8620 Ironwood Ave.
Dallas, TX 75204

_____ 19 ____ $\frac{60\text{-}105}{313}$

PAY TO THE
ORDER OF _____ $ _____

_____ DOLLARS

AGS National Bank

MEMO _____   _____

⑈■0 0333 2 ⑈■ ■■0 5 2 0 0 0 6 1 8 ⑈■

Check Stubs

A *check stub* is used to keep a record of the deposits and checks written. The *balance* tells the amount of money in the account. Deposits are added to the account; checks written are subtracted. If there is a *service charge* for each check, it is also subtracted.

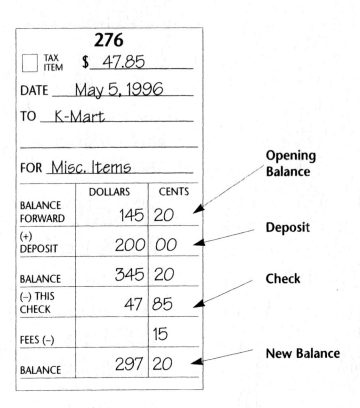

Example:

Christa's account has a balance of $145.20. After she makes a deposit of $200.00 and writes a check for $47.85, what is the balance in her account? There is a $.15 service charge for each check.

The new balance is $297.20.

A Find the new balance for each check and/or deposit.

1.

	DOLLARS	CENTS
BALANCE FORWARD	175	50
(+) DEPOSIT		
BALANCE		
(–)THIS CHECK	42	85
FEES (–)		15
BALANCE		

2.

	DOLLARS	CENTS
BALANCE FORWARD	214	83
(+) DEPOSIT	400	00
BALANCE		
(–)THIS CHECK	18	25
FEES (–)		15
BALANCE		

3.

	DOLLARS	CENTS
BALANCE FORWARD	628	50
(+) DEPOSIT		
BALANCE		
(–)THIS CHECK	175	14
FEES (–)		15
BALANCE		

4.

	DOLLARS	CENTS
BALANCE FORWARD	902	83
(+) DEPOSIT	100	00
BALANCE		
(–)THIS CHECK	186	14
FEES (–)		15
BALANCE		

B Use the check stubs to answer the questions.

5. What was the opening balance on July 1? _____

6. To whom was check #277 written? _____

7. For how much was the check? _____

8. For what was check #277 written? _____

9. What was the closing balance on July 1? _____

10. Was a fee recorded for the check? _____

277		
☐ TAX ITEM $ 25.50		
DATE 7/1/96		
TO Barlow Florists		
FOR Flowers		
	DOLLARS	CENTS
BALANCE FORWARD	275	12
(+) DEPOSIT	—	
BALANCE	275	12
(–) THIS CHECK	25	50
FEES (–)	—	
BALANCE		

11. What was the opening balance on July 3? _____

12. How much was deposited on July 3? _____

13. What was the balance after the deposit? _____

14. For what was check #278 written? _____

15. For how much was the check? _____

16. Was a fee recorded for the check? _____

17. What was the closing balance on July 3? _____

278		
☐ TAX ITEM $ 45.72		
DATE 7/3/96		
TO Holland Auto		
FOR Car repairs		
	DOLLARS	CENTS
BALANCE FORWARD		
(+) DEPOSIT	125	00
BALANCE		
(–) THIS CHECK	45	72
FEES (–)	—	
BALANCE		

C Complete each check stub and carry the balance forward.

18. Check Number: 802

	DOLLARS	CENTS
BALANCE FORWARD	475	26
(+) DEPOSIT	400	00
BALANCE		
(–)THIS CHECK	125	50
FEES (–)	—	
BALANCE		

19. Check Number: 803

	DOLLARS	CENTS
BALANCE FORWARD		
(+) DEPOSIT	—	
BALANCE		
(–)THIS CHECK	32	15
FEES (–)	—	
BALANCE		

20. Check Number: 804

	DOLLARS	CENTS
BALANCE FORWARD		
(+) DEPOSIT	—	
BALANCE		
(–)THIS CHECK	205	00
FEES (–)	—	
BALANCE		

Running Balance, Part 1

A *running balance* is a continuous record of how much is in your checking account. It includes all deposits and checks written.

Example: Fred's opening balance is $625.40. He makes a deposit of $250.00 and writes a check for $115.50. What is his balance at the end of the day?

			802

TAX ITEM		802
	$ 115.50	
DATE	8/26/96	
TO	Ross Plumbers	
FOR	Repair	

	DOLLARS	CENTS
BALANCE FORWARD	625	40
(+) DEPOSIT	250	00
BALANCE	875	40
(−) THIS CHECK	115	50
FEES (−)		
BALANCE	759	90

FRED ALLEN
22 LAUREL DRIVE
UNION, NJ 07087

8/26 19 96   7-89 / 520

PAY TO THE ORDER OF Ross Plumbers $ 115.50

One hundred fifteen and 50/100 ———————— DOLLARS

AGSNational Bank

MEMO repair hot water heater   Fred Allen

‖ ■ 0 0333 2 ‖ ■ ■ ■ 0 5 2 0 0 0 6 1 8 ‖ ■   0 03 333 2 2 ‖ ■

His balance at the end of the day is $759.90.

Complete each check and stub and carry the balance forward. The opening balance is $525.15.

Date	Deposits	Check#	Payee	For	Amount
5/2/98		147	Atkins Lumber Co.	Lumber	$75.62
5/4/98	$175.00	148	Giant Foods	Food	$48.16
5/5/98		149	Dr. John Lavin	Doctor's Visit	$25.00

Check 147

TAX ITEM	$ _____	147

DATE _____
TO _____
_____
FOR _____

	DOLLARS	CENTS
BALANCE FORWARD		
(+) DEPOSIT		
BALANCE (–) THIS CHECK		
FEES (–)		
BALANCE		

FRAN WELLS
15 PINE LANE
HINSDALE, IL 60521

147

_____ 19 ____   7-89
                        ─────
                        520

PAY TO THE
ORDER OF _____ $ _____

_____ DOLLARS

AGSNational Bank

MEMO _____   _____

‖■ 0 0333 2 ‖■ ■■ 0 5 2 0 0 0 6 1 8 ‖■   0 04 333 2 2 ‖■

Check 148

TAX ITEM	$ _____	148

DATE _____
TO _____
_____
FOR _____

	DOLLARS	CENTS
BALANCE FORWARD		
(+) DEPOSIT		
BALANCE (–) THIS CHECK		
FEES (–)		
BALANCE		

FRAN WELLS
15 PINE LANE
HINSDALE, IL 60521

148

_____ 19 ____   7-89
                        ─────
                        520

PAY TO THE
ORDER OF _____ $ _____

_____ DOLLARS

AGSNational Bank

MEMO _____   _____

‖■ 0 0333 2 ‖■ ■■ 0 5 2 0 0 0 6 1 8 ‖■   0 04 333 2 2 ‖■

Check 149

TAX ITEM	$ _____	149

DATE _____
TO _____
_____
FOR _____

	DOLLARS	CENTS
BALANCE FORWARD		
(+) DEPOSIT		
BALANCE (–) THIS CHECK		
FEES (–)		
BALANCE		

FRAN WELLS
15 PINE LANE
HINSDALE, IL 60521

149

_____ 19 ____

PAY TO THE
ORDER OF _____ $ _____

_____ DOLLARS

AGSNational Bank

MEMO _____   _____

‖■ 0 0333 2 ‖■ ■■ 0 5 2 0 0 0 6 1 8 ‖■   0 04 333 2 2 ‖■

Running Balance, Part 2

 Complete each check and stub and carry the balance forward. The opening balance is $728.32.

Date	Deposits	Check#	Payee	For	Amount
9/2/97		726	Harris's Market	Food	$68.75
9/3/97	$125.00	727	G. & R. Books	Books	$24.15
9/6/97		728	Carroll Co. Bank	Car payment	$210.00
9/10/97	$450.00	729	Gas Company	Utilities	$165.25
9/11/97		730	Willis's Garage	Car repair	$78.65

726

☐ TAX ITEM $_____

DATE _____

TO _____

_____

FOR _____

	DOLLARS	CENTS
BALANCE FORWARD		
(+) DEPOSIT		
BALANCE (–) THIS CHECK		
FEES (–)		
BALANCE		

MARIA CHAVEZ
32 REED ROAD
NASHVILLE, TN 37013

726

_____ 19 _____   7-89 / 520

PAY TO THE
ORDER OF _____ $ _____

_____ DOLLARS

AGSNational Bank

MEMO _____   _____

‖ ■ 0 0333 2 ‖ ■ ■ ■ 0 5 2 0 0 0 6 1 8 ‖ ■   0 05   333 2 2 ‖ ■

727

☐ TAX ITEM $_____

DATE _____

TO _____

_____

FOR _____

	DOLLARS	CENTS
BALANCE FORWARD		
(+) DEPOSIT		
BALANCE (–) THIS CHECK		
FEES (–)		
BALANCE		

MARIA CHAVEZ
32 REED ROAD
NASHVILLE, TN 37013

727

_____ 19 _____   7-89 / 520

PAY TO THE
ORDER OF _____ $ _____

_____ DOLLARS

AGSNational Bank

MEMO _____   _____

‖ ■ 0 0333 2 ‖ ■ ■ ■ 0 5 2 0 0 0 6 1 8 ‖ ■   0 05   333 2 2 ‖ ■

Check 728

		728
TAX ITEM ☐	$ _____	

DATE _____

TO _____

_____

FOR _____

	DOLLARS	CENTS
BALANCE FORWARD		
(+) DEPOSIT		
BALANCE (–) THIS CHECK		
FEES (–)		
BALANCE		

MARIA CHAVEZ
32 REED ROAD
NASHVILLE, TN 37013

_____ 19 _____   7-89 / 520

PAY TO THE
ORDER OF _____ $ _____

_____ DOLLARS

AGSNational Bank

MEMO _____

‖■ 0 0333 2 ‖■ ■■ 0 5 2 0 0 0 6 1 8 ‖■   0 03 333 2 2 ‖■

Check 729

		729
TAX ITEM ☐	$ _____	

DATE _____

TO _____

_____

FOR _____

	DOLLARS	CENTS
BALANCE FORWARD		
(+) DEPOSIT		
BALANCE (–) THIS CHECK		
FEES (–)		
BALANCE		

MARIA CHAVEZ
32 REED ROAD
NASHVILLE, TN 37013

_____ 19 _____   7-89 / 520

PAY TO THE
ORDER OF _____ $ _____

_____ DOLLARS

AGSNational Bank

MEMO _____

‖■ 0 0333 2 ‖■ ■ ■■ 0 5 2 0 0 0 6 1 8 ‖■   0 03 333 2 2 ‖■

Check 730

		730
TAX ITEM ☐	$ _____	

DATE _____

TO _____

_____

FOR _____

	DOLLARS	CENTS
BALANCE FORWARD		
(+) DEPOSIT		
BALANCE (–) THIS CHECK		
FEES (–)		
BALANCE		

MARIA CHAVEZ
32 REED ROAD
NASHVILLE, TN 37013

_____ 19 _____   7-89 / 520

PAY TO THE
ORDER OF _____ $ _____

_____ DOLLARS

AGSNational Bank

MEMO _____

‖■ 0 0333 2 ‖■ ■ ■■ 0 5 2 0 0 0 6 1 8 ‖■   0 03 333 2 2 ‖■

Consumer Checkpoint 1

 Solve each problem. Then circle the letter of the correct answer.

1. Sonia Perez earns $540 for a 40-hour week. If her overtime pay is 1.5 times her straight-time rate, how much does Sonia earn for each overtime hour she works?

   a. $13.50   **b.** $6.75   **c.** $20.25   **d.** $22.50

2. Tonya earns $7.40 per hour; Glenn earns $6.95 per hour; Julie earns $7.25 per hour; and Larry earns $8.05 per hour. Which employee earns $290 per 40-hour week?

   a. Larry   **b.** Tonya   **c.** Glenn   **d.** Julie

3. A computer technician's gross pay is $640.20 per week. His deductions total $201.38. What is his net pay?

   a. $438.82   **b.** $640.20   **c.** $841.58   **d.** $458.82

4. Rob's opening balance was $1,421.11. He deposited checks for $74.00, $864.10, and $250.00. Then he withdrew $300 in cash. What is his current balance?

   a. $233.01   **b.** $2,000.91   **c.** $2,309.21   **d.** $2,609.21

5. Tuan deposited $1,500 in a savings account that pays an annual rate of 7% interest compounded semiannually. Adela deposited $1,500 in a savings account that pays 8% interest annually. How much more money will Adela have than Tuan at the end of 1 year?

   a. $13.16   **b.** $15.76   **c.** $97.35   **d.** $102.20

6. Liz deposited $1,200 in a savings account that paid $5\frac{1}{4}$% annually. How much would Liz have in her account after 1 year?

   a. $1,263.00   **b.** $1,830.00   **c.** $1,260.00   **d.** $1,206.30

7. What is the simple interest on $2,500 for 6 months at $9\frac{1}{2}$%?

   a. $150.00   **b.** $237.50   **c.** $112.50   **d.** $118.75

8. Dan earned $426.40 last week. His deductions totaled $102.25. What was his net pay?

   a. $528.65   **b.** $314.15   **c.** $324.15   **d.** $334.15

9. Jake earns $4.50 an hour and 10% on all sales over $1,000. Last week he worked 36 hours and sold $4,600 worth of merchandise. What was Jake's gross pay?

   a. $162.00   **b.** $622.00   **c.** $460.00   **d.** $522.00

10. The Happy Home Realty Company sold the Parkers' home for $178,400. The commission rate was $6\frac{3}{4}$%. How much did the Parkers receive from the sale of their home?

    a. $11,310.56   **b.** $57,980.00   **c.** $166,358.00   **d.** $160,358.00

Multiplication of Decimals

Rules to Remember:

To multiply two decimal fractions:

➤ Multiply the same as whole numbers.

➤ Count the number of places to the right of the decimal point in both factors.

➤ Beginning at the right, count the same number of decimal places in the product.

➤ Place the decimal point.

➤ Sometimes it is necessary to insert zeros in the product.

Examples:

Multiply: 6.7 x 2.35   Multiply: 2.7 x .063

```
   2.35  ◄— 2 places          .063  ◄— 3 places
 x 6.7   ◄— 1 place         x .27   ◄— 2 places
  1645                        441
 1410                         126
 15.745  ◄— 3 places        .01701  ◄— 5 places
```
Place decimal point.   **Insert zero.**

A Multiply. Check your answers.

1. 27.5	2. 16.34	3. .07	4. 17.5	5. 28.3	6. 172
x 8	x 12	x 82	x 4.2	x .05	x .45

7. 67.3	8. .723	9. .027	10. 1.76	11. .273	12. 1.872
x 1.4	x .17	x 5	x .003	x .76	x .008

B Multiply. Check your answers.

13. 27.50 x 16 = _____   14. 45.16 x 26 = _____

15. 1.76 x 8.3 = _____   16. .073 x 18 = _____

17. .072 x .05 = _____   18. .178 x .024 = _____

Salespeople in some stores help count the stock on hand once a month. This process is called *taking inventory*. The inventory also gives the value of the merchandise. To find the value, multiply the *unit cost* by the number of items.

Example: At the end of the season, the Sea Side Scuba Shop had 4 underwater cameras valued at $120 each and 12 diving suits valued at $89.95 each in stock. What is the value of the Scuba Shop's inventory?

Inventory Value = Unit Cost x Number of Items
= ($120 x 4) + ($89.95 x 12)
= $480.00 + $1,079.40
= $1,559.40

The value of the Scuba Shop's inventory is $1,559.40.

C Find the value of the inventory for each item.

Items	Inventory	Unit Cost	Value
19. Camera bags	12	$24.50	
20. Zoom lenses	16	89.90	
21. Electronic flashes	10	65.25	
22. Disposable cameras	23	6.50	
23. Tripods	18	37.75	
24. Slide viewers	20	18.65	
25. Pocket cameras	6	58.90	
26. "AA" batteries	2,100	.59	
27. Deluxe camera bags	7	57.75	
28. Camera film	250	4.75	
29. 35mm cameras	9	349.90	
30. Photo albums	15	22.00	
31. Telephoto lenses	4	96.25	
32. Light filters	17	13.40	

Parts of a Budget

A *budget* is a plan for spending and saving money. A well-planned budget is the key to wise spending and saving.

Example: Mark has a part-time job in a gas station. His monthly net income is $300. This is his monthly budget:

Items	% of Budget	Amount
Savings	10%	$30.00
Car: Gas, Oil, Insurance	30%	1.
Entertainment, Dates	30%	2.
Clothing	15%	3.
Gifts, Contributions	10%	4.
Personal Items	5%	5.
		TOTAL $300.00

How much did Mark set aside for savings in his budget?

Amount	=	% of budget	x	Net income

    =   .10   x $300.00
    = $30.00

Mark plans to save $30.00 a month.

A Find the amount budgeted for all of the other items in Mark's budget and record them on the chart.

B Missy has a part-time job as a salesclerk. She has a monthly net income of $360.00. Find the amount budgeted for each item in her budget.

Items	% of Budget	Amount
Transportation	20%	6.
Food	8%	7.
Clothing	25%	8.
Telephone	5%	9.
Personal Items	5%	10.
Gifts, Contributions	10%	11.
Entertainment	12%	12.
Savings	15%	13.
		TOTAL $360.00

C Walter and Karen are newlyweds. They have a monthly net income of $3,800. Find the amount set aside for each item in their budget.

Items	% of Budget	Amount
Food	20%	14.
Housing	23%	15.
Clothing	15%	16.
Insurance	2%	17.
Utilities	5%	18.
Personal Items	8%	19.
Entertainment	7%	20.
Transportation	14%	21.
Savings	6%	22.
		TOTAL $3,800.00

Preparing a Budget

The first step in managing your money is to keep a record of how you spend it. At the end of three months, you will be in a better position to determine your spending habits.

Example: Miguel has a part-time job that pays him a monthly net income of $250.00. Miguel's expenditures for the last three months are shown below.

Items	Sept.	Oct.	Nov.	Average Expenditure
Food	$22	$25	$28	$25.00
Transportation	100	40	70	1.
Entertainment	25	45	20	2.
Personal Items	28	25	19	3.
Gifts, Contributions	15	10	20	4.
Clothing	50	45	40	5.
Savings	10	60	53	6.
Totals	**$250**	**$250**	**$250**	**$250.00**

What was Miguel's average expenditure for food?

Average expenditure = Sum of monthly expenditures ÷ Number of months
= ($22 + 25 + 28) ÷ 3
= $75 ÷ 3
= $25.00

Miguel's average expenditure for food is $25.00.

A Find the average expenditure for each item in Miguel's budget and record it on the chart.

This is a record of how the Johnsons spent their net income for the last four months. Their average expenditure for rent was $950.00.

B Find the average expenditure for the other items in their budget.

Budget Items	March	April	May	June	Avg. Expenditure
Rent	$950	$950	$950	$950	$950
Food	700	700	690	720	7.
Clothing	400	600	360	440	8.
Transportation	380	380	380	380	9.
Entertainment	185	200	150	225	10.
Insurance	250	250	450	250	11.
Utilities	300	220	180	160	12.
Telephone	60	75	60	58	13.
Personal Items	200	250	180	220	14.
Contributions	100	140	120	117	15.
Savings	475	235	480	480	16.
Total Spendings	$4,000	$4,000	$4,000	$4,000	$4,000

17. How much did the Johnsons spend in March? _____
18. What is the average monthly expenditure for food? _____
19. What is the average monthly expenditure for clothing? _____
20. How much is the monthly transportation expense for the Johnsons? _____
21. Items that stay the same in a budget are called *fixed* expenses. What items are fixed in their budget? _____
22. What month has the highest amount budgeted for insurance? _____
23. What month has the highest amount budgeted for clothing? _____
24. How much do the Johnsons save each month on an average? _____
25. If the Johnsons want to be sure they save an additional $50.00 a month, on what items might they spend less? _____

Comparing Budgets

Everyone's budget is not the same. A personal budget should be based on individual needs and income. For example, the transportation expenses for a person who has to make monthly payments on a car would be different from those of one who rides public transportation.

Example: Margaret and Robert both have part-time jobs. Margaret's monthly income is $240, and Robert's is $200. Their individual needs are shown in their budgets.

What percent did each spend for food?

Margaret:

Percent spent = Amount spent ÷ Total budget
= $12.00 ÷ $240.00
= .05 = 5%

Robert:

Percent spent = Amount spent ÷ Total budget
= $20.00 ÷ $200.00
= .10 = 10%

	Margaret's Budget			Robert's Budget	
Items	**Amount**	**Percent**		**Amount**	**Percent**
Clothing	$96.00	1. _____		$30.00	7. _____
Transportation	12.00	2. _____		60.00	8. _____
Entertainment	24.00	3. _____		50.00	9. _____
Gifts, Contributions	48.00	4. _____		20.00	10. _____
Personal Items	36.00	5. _____		10.00	11. _____
Savings	12.00	6. _____		10.00	12. _____
Food	12.00	5%		20.00	10%
	$240.00			**$200.00**	

A Find the percent spent for each item in Margaret's and Robert's budgets.

13. What is the largest item in Margaret's budget? _____

14. What is the largest item in Robert's budget? _____

Ralph has a monthly net income of $4,000. Joseph's monthly net income is $1,500. Their budgets are shown below.

B Find the percent spent for each item in Ralph's and Joseph's budgets.

	Ralph's Budget		Joseph's Budget	
Items	**Amount**	**Percent**	**Amount**	**Percent**
Rent	$900.00	15. _____	$500.00	25. _____
Food	600.00	16. _____	300.00	26. _____
Clothing	400.00	17. _____	75.00	27. _____
Transportation	250.00	18. _____	150.00	28. _____
Insurance	250.00	19. _____	60.00	29. _____
Entertainment	200.00	20. _____	120.00	30. _____
Personal Items	180.00	21. _____	25.00	31. _____
Gifts, Contributions	220.00	22. _____	90.00	32. _____
Utilities and Phone	200.00	23. _____	150.00	33. _____
Savings	800.00	24. _____	30.00	34. _____
	$4,000.00		**$1,500.00**	

35. What is the largest item in Ralph's budget? _____

36. What is the largest item in Joseph's budget? _____

37. What is the smallest item in Ralph's budget? _____

38. What is the smallest item in Joseph's budget? _____

39. Who budgets the most for rent? _____

40. What is the difference between the amounts budgeted for savings? _____

41. What is the difference between the amounts budgeted for food? _____

42. What is the difference between the amounts budgeted for clothing? _____

Multiplying by 10, 100, and 1,000

Rules to Remember:

To multiply by 10, 100, or 1,000, move the decimal point to the right.

➤ To multiply by 10, move the decimal point *one* place to the right; by 100, *two* places to the right; by 1,000, *three* places to the right.

➤ When necessary, add zeros to have the correct number of decimal places.

Examples:

Multiply: 4.75 x 10
4.75 x 10 = 47.5

Multiply: 7.3 x 1,000
7.3 x 1,000 = 7300

Add two zeros

 **A** Multiply by 10.

1. 7.5   2. 12.86   3. .172   4. 72   5. 12.68

_____   _____   _____   _____   _____

B Multiply by 100.

6. 8.36   7. 9.025   8. 12.6   9. 48   10. .763

_____   _____   _____   _____   _____

C Multiply by 1,000.

11. 7.263   12. .075   13. 9.3   14. 274   15. 12.7283

_____   _____   _____   _____   _____

D Multiply.

16. 82.3 x 100   17. 19.5 x 10   18. 129.72 x 1,000

_____   _____   _____

Rules to Remember:

Percent means hundredths.

To change a decimal to a percent:

➤ Move the decimal point two places to the right.

➤ Add a percent sign.

To change a percent to a decimal:

➤ Move the decimal point two places to the left.

➤ Drop the percent sign.

Examples:

Write a percent for .85.
.85 = .85 = 85%

Write a percent for .075.
.075 = .075 = 7.5%

Write a decimal for 27%.
27% = 27% = .27

Write a decimal for 5.4%.
5.4% = 05.4% = .054

A Write a decimal for each percent.

1. 45% _____   2. 90% _____

3. 4% _____   4. 18.5% _____

5. 25% _____   6. $7\frac{3}{4}$% _____

7. 7.5% _____   8. 12.55% _____

9. $8\frac{1}{2}$% _____   10. .5% _____

B Write a percent for each decimal.

11. .72 _____   12. .125 _____

13. .65 _____   14. .1125 _____

15. .05 _____   16. .375 _____

17. .065 _____ 18. .082 _____

19. .045 _____ 20. .1265 _____

Credit Cards

When you buy something and agree to pay for it at a later date, or make regular payments until it is paid for, you are using *credit*. The most popular form of credit is using a *credit card*.

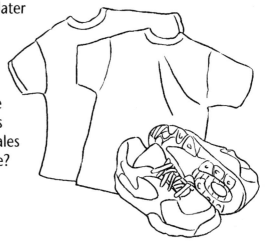

Example: Joel Raedeke purchased some items at the SeaQuest Shop. He paid for them with his credit card. The salesclerk prepared this sales receipt. What was the total purchase price?

4342 170 802 061   **5688289**

08/89 CV

JOEL RAEDEKE

403 001 487
291 105 133 3
SEAQUEST SHOP 141

SALES SLIP
THIS FORM TO BE USED WITH

SAFE/PERF U.S. Pat. 4,403,793

QTY	CLASS	DESCRIPTION	PRICE	AMOUNT
1		Shorts	12.75	12 75
2		Shirts	10.75	21 50
1		Belt	10.95	10 95

DATE 5/28	AUTHORIZATION NO.	CLERK TG	DEPT.	SUB TOTAL	45 20

Cardholder acknowledges receipt of goods and/or services in the amount of the Total shown hereon and agrees to perform the obligations set forth in the Cardholder's agreement with the issuer. — **TAX** | 2 26

CUSTOMER SIGNATURE

X *Joel Raedeke*   **TOTAL**

CUSTOMER COPY   **IMPORTANT: RETAIN THIS COPY FOR YOUR RECORDS.**

Total purchase price = Total sales + Sales tax

= $45.20 + $2.26

= $47.46

The total purchase price is $47.46.

A Compute the total sales, sales tax, and total purchase price.

	Total Purchases	Total Sales	Sales Tax Rate	Sales Tax	Purchase Price
1.	$17.25; $8.40		5%		
2.	$48.60; $19.20		5%		
3.	$128.50		4%		
4.	$45.60; $27.90		7%		
5.	$16.75; $90.85		6%		
6.	$14.72; $8.65; $9.28		5%		
7.	$285.00		4%		
8.	$84.12; $103.38		7%		
9.	$62.50; $19.25		4%		
10.	$145.60; $82.40		5%		

B Complete the sales receipts.

11. Joan Rivera purchased some stationery and a pen and pencil set. The sales tax rate is 4%.

QTY	CLASS	DESCRIPTION	PRICE	AMOUNT
		stationery		25 50
		Pen and pencil		18 75

DATE	AUTHORIZATION NO.	CLERK	DEPT.	SUB TOTAL	

Cardholder acknowledges receipt of goods and/or services in the amount of the Total shown hereon and agrees to perform the obligations set forth in the Cardholder's agreement with the issuer. **TAX**

CUSTOMER SIGNATURE
X **TOTAL**

QTY	CLASS	DESCRIPTION	PRICE	AMOUNT
1		Power saw		49 95
1		Power drill		29 95

DATE	AUTHORIZATION NO.	CLERK	DEPT.	SUB TOTAL	

Cardholder acknowledges receipt of goods and/or services in the amount of the Total shown hereon and agrees to perform the obligations set forth in the Cardholder's agreement with the issuer. **TAX**

CUSTOMER SIGNATURE
X **TOTAL**

12. Robert Murray purchased some tools. The sales tax rate is 4%.

QTY	CLASS	DESCRIPTION	PRICE	AMOUNT
10		Paint brushes	2.55	25 50
20		Bottles of paint	1.50	30 00

DATE	AUTHORIZATION NO.	CLERK	DEPT.	SUB TOTAL	

Cardholder acknowledges receipt of goods and/or services in the amount of the Total shown hereon and agrees to perform the obligations set forth in the Cardholder's agreement with the issuer. **TAX**

CUSTOMER SIGNATURE
X **TOTAL**

13. Mary Upland bought art supplies. The sales tax rate is 5%.

Finance Charges

Once a month, persons who have charge cards receive a statement of the balance due on their account. When you do not pay the full amount due, you have to pay a *finance charge*.

Example: Cindy's unpaid balance from last month is $125.50. This month her purchases totaled $85.70, and she made a $50.00 payment. The finance charge was $2.25. What is the new balance on her account?

New balance	=	Previous balance	+	New purchases	+	Finance charge	–	Payment

$$= (\$125.50 + \$85.70 + \$2.25) - \$50.00$$
$$= \$213.45 - \$50.00$$
$$= \$163.45$$

The new balance is $163.45.

A Use a calculator to find the new balance.

1.
Monthly Statement
    for Harry Williams
Previous balance: $175.80
New purchases: $17.60; $25.40
Finance charge: $2.15
Payment: $50.00

_____

2.
Monthly Statement
    for Monica Hernandez
Previous balance: $752.40
New purchases: $42.77; $34.20; $25.70
Finance charge: $18.14
Payment: $70.00

_____

3.
Monthly Statement
    for Latoya Wilson
Previous balance: $623.45
New purchases: $38.20; $25; $55
Finance charge: $16.23
Payment: $80.00

_____

4.
Monthly Statement
    for Will Jones
Previous balance: $875.20
New purchases: $27.60; $18.25; $42.60
Finance charge: $23.62
Payment: $95.00

_____

B Complete the table.

	Previous Balance	New Purchases	Finance Charge	Payment	New Balance
5.	$85.26	$46.50	$1.28	$50.00	
6.	126.40	86.90	1.85	75.00	
7.	472.80	90.60	7.15	100.00	
8.	91.50	100.75	1.35	50.00	
9.	1,726.40	225.17	25.43	200.00	
10.	75.90	84.28	1.02	75.00	
11.	3,276.12	475.90	48.16	350.00	
12.	876.45	216.80	13.28	250.00	
13.	1,076.18	195.62	15.72	200.00	
14.	612.92	215.60	9.17	100.00	
15.	485.90	142.80	7.20	35.00	
16.	2,072.15	295.76	30.16	175.00	

C Fill in the new balance for each credit statement.

17.
Previous Balance: $724.60
Purchases: $126.90
Payment: $150.00
New Balance:
Finance Charge: $10.40

18.
Previous Balance: $92.75
Purchases: $121.40
Payment: $75.00
New Balance:
Finance Charge: $1.37

19.
Previous Balance: $2,736.12
Purchases: $425.08
Payment: $200.00
New Balance:
Finance Charge: $40.28

20.
Previous Balance: $1,076.28
Purchases: $316.92
Payment: $450.00
New Balance:
Finance Charge: $16.27

Installment Buying

Some costly items are sold on an *installment plan*. Instead of paying the full price of the item at the time of purchase, only a part of the price is paid. This is called the *down payment*. The remainder is paid in *monthly installments*. Like all credit purchasing, a *finance charge* is added to the cost of what you buy.

Example: Martha purchased a $425.00 television set. She had to pay 10% down and make 12 monthly installments of $35.00. What is the installment price? What is the finance charge?

Down payment	=	Cash price	x	% down

$$= \$425.00 \times .10$$

$$= \$42.50$$

Installment price	=	Down payment	+	Total installment payments

$$= \$42.50 + (12 \times \$35.00)$$

$$= \$42.50 + \$420.00$$

$$= \$462.50$$

The installment price is $462.50.

Finance charge	=	Installment price	–	Cash price

$$= \$462.50 - \$425.00$$

$$= \$37.50$$

The finance charge is $37.50.

A Find the installment price and finance charge for each.

	Item	Cash Price	Down Payment	No. of Payments	Monthly Installments	Installment Price	Finance Charge
1.	Refrigerator	$575	$60	12	$55.25		
2.	VCR	375	75	6	57.20		
3.	Color TV	415	75	12	34.75		
4.	Air conditioner	380	52	9	42.00		
5.	Rug	750	100	18	40.25		
6.	CD player	125	35	6	16.75		
7.	Lawn mower	385	75	24	15.00		
8.	Dishwasher	425	125	12	29.25		
9.	Boat	3,500	500	36	95.00		
10.	Camper	5,000	900	48	97.50		
11.	Lawn furniture	765	95	18	41.20		
12.	Camera	295	50	6	49.75		

B Find the down payment and the amount financed.

	Item	Cash Price	Rate of Payment	Down Payment	Amount Financed
13.	Oven	$625	10%		
14.	Color TV	485	20%		
15.	VCR	315	20%		
16.	Sewing machine	487	15%		
17.	Video camera	730	20%		
18.	Kitchen set	815	25%		
19.	Sofa	650	12%		
20.	Bed	175	30%		

Short-Term Loans

Sometimes you need to borrow money for a short time to pay taxes, make car repairs, or take a vacation. For the privilege of borrowing the money, there is a *finance charge*.

Example: Scott Jones plans to take a vacation to Europe. He borrows $1,500, which he plans to pay back in 6 monthly payments of $265.50. How much does he have to pay back? What is the finance charge?

Amount to be paid back	=	Amount of monthly payment	x	Number of months

$$= \ \$265.50 \times 6$$

$$= \ \$1,593.00$$

The amount to be paid back is $1,593.00.

Finance charge	=	Amount paid back	–	Amount borrowed

$$= \ \$1,593.00 - \$1,500.00$$

$$= \ \$93.00$$

The finance charge is $93.00.

Find the amount to be repaid and the finance charge.

1. Stan Smith

   Borrowed $2,000

   Repaid: $355.20 in

   6 monthly payments

   Amount repaid? _____

   Finance charge? _____

2. Tom Foster

   Borrowed $1,750

   Repaid: $164.25 in

   12 monthly payments

   Amount repaid? _____

   Finance charge? _____

	Purpose	Amount Borrowed	No. of Payments	Monthly Payment	Amount Repaid	Finance Charge
3.	New appliance	$600	6	$112.50		
4.	Home repairs	2,500	18	163.85		
5.	Business loan	1,750	12	164.70		
6.	Hospital bill	4,000	24	204.25		
7.	Insurance	850	12	79.60		
8.	Tuition	4,500	20	269.75		
9.	Taxes	3,750	24	187.50		
10.	Car purchase	4,800	36	173.35		
11.	Roof repair	3,450	6	680.65		
12.	Vacation	2,650	18	174.10		
13.	Dental bill	1,200	10	134.00		
14.	Taxes	6,150	20	370.50		
15.	Car repair	900	12	80.30		

 Bill Gerardi borrowed $1,750 to build a deck. A finance charge of $175 was added to the amount he had to repay. If he pays off the loan in ten monthly payments, how much is each payment?

_____

Finding a Percent of a Number

Rules to Remember:

To find a percent of a number:

➤ Write a decimal or a fraction for the percent.

➤ Multiply.

Examples:

Find 45% of 180.   180
45% = .45   x .45   45% of 180 = 81
                   900
                   720
                  81.00

Find $33\frac{1}{3}$% of 279. $\frac{1}{3}$ x $\frac{\overset{93}{\cancel{279}}}{1}$ = 93

$33\frac{1}{3}$% = $\frac{1}{3}$ $33\frac{1}{3}$% of 279 = 93 $33\frac{1}{3}$ = $\frac{1}{3}$

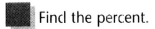 Find the percent.

1. 25% of 48 _____

2. 40% of 65 _____

3. 90% of 70 _____

4. 16% of 85 _____

5. 3% of 68 _____

6. 12% of 250 _____

7. 7.5% of 60 _____

8. 36% of 72.5 _____

9. 1.4% of 250 _____

10. 12.5% of 80 _____

11. $33\frac{1}{3}$% of 27 _____

12. $66\frac{2}{3}$% of 123 _____

13. 72% of 45 _____

14. 90% of 128 _____

15. 5% of 140 _____

16. 37.5% of 64 _____

17. 4.5% of 600 _____

18. 12.5% of 48 _____

Pgs 41-60

her:

or.

Find _____% of 540 = 24.3

oduct   Factor   Product

```
        .6u                              .045
    60)36.00                        540)24.300
      360                               2160
        0                               2700
                                        2700
                                           0
```

60% of 60 = 36   4.5% of 540 = 24.3

Solve the percent problems.

1. _____% of 50 = 25   2. _____% of 24 = 18

3. _____% of 40 = 24   4. _____% of 15 = 3

5. 40 = _____% of 80   6. 25 = _____% of 100

7. _____% of 45 = 9   8. _____% of 50 = 20

9. _____% of 50 = 3   10. _____% of 64 = 16

11. 12 = _____% of 40   12. 25 = _____% of 80

13. _____% of 20 = 19   14. _____% of 9 = 2.7

15. _____% of 60 = 15   16. _____% of 72 = 36

17. _____% of 25 = 18   18. _____% of 40 = 1

19. 16 = _____% of 50   20. 40 = _____% of 75

On the side window of a new car, you will see a sticker that shows the charges for the car. The *base price* is the price for standard equipment. Extras for convenience, safety, or appearance, such as air conditioning, tinted glass, or power windows, are called *options*. The *destination charge* is the cost of shipping the car from the factory to the dealer. The price of the car is called the *sticker price.* It is the sum of the base price, options, and destination charge.

Example: Carol Jones is shopping for a new compact car. The sticker on one of the cars she looked at is shown below. Find the sticker price.

	$15,600.00
OPTIONS DESCRIPTION	**List Price**
V-6 Engine	$550.00
Automatic Transmission	640.00
Power Windows	350.00
AM/FM Stereo w/Cassette	170.00
Air Conditioning	840.00
Body Paint Stripe	55.00
DESTINATION CHARGE	525.00

Total options = $550 + $640 + $350 + $170 + $840 + $55

= $2,605.00

Sticker price = Base price + Options + Destination charge

= $15,600.00 + $2,605.00 + $525.00

= $18,730.00

The sticker price is $18,730.00.

Find the sticker price.

1. compact car

   Base price: $13,399

   Options: $1,955

   Destination charge: $490

   Sticker price _____

2. 2-door convertible

   Base price: $18,305

   Options: $1,255

   Destination charge: $475

   Sticker price _____

3. sedan

   Base price: $15,895

   Options:

   　automatic transmission, $200

   　air conditioner, $830

   　tinted glass, $245

   Destination charge: $530

   Sticker price _____

4. sport vehicle

   Base price: $14,400

   Options:

   　AM/FM stereo, $275

   　roof rack, $139

   　automatic transmission, $394

   　metallic paint, $173

   Destination charge: $495

   Sticker price _____

	Base Price	Options	Destination Charge	Sticker Price
5.	$11,295	$1,975	$240	
6.	8,250	1,645	175	
7.	10,495	2,095	250	
8.	7,825	2,465	217	
9.	8,975	1,900	315	
10.	12,525	3,365	290	
11.	8,105	1,765	165	
12.	5,485	2,135	295	
13.	8,450	3,150	200	
14.	8,725	1,785	325	
15.	11,275	4,675	385	
16.	10,075	3,415	210	

Buying a Used Car **Lesson 2**

New and used cars are advertised in the newspaper. The price you see in the paper is not the *total cost.* Besides the list price, the total cost includes *sales tax, title fee,* and a *license plate fee.*

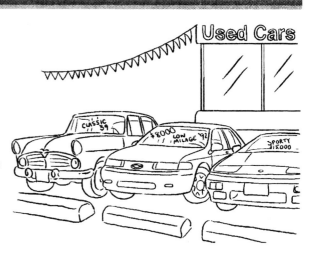

Example: Malcolm Carter buys a used car for $4,550. The sales tax is 5% of the price of the car. The title fee is $8.00, and the license plate fee is $25.00. What is the total cost of the car?

Sales tax = Price of car x Sales tax rate

= $4,550 x .05

= $227.50

Total cost = Price of car + Sales tax + Title fee + License plate fee

= $4,550.00 + $227.50 + $8.00 + $25.00

= $4,810.50

The total cost of the car is $4,810.50.

A   Find the total cost of the car.

1. List price: $3,800

   Sales tax rate: 4%

   Title fee: $27.50

   License plate fee: $17.50

   Total cost _____

2. List price: $2,495

   Sales tax rate: 6%

   Title fee: $12.50

   License plate fee: $25.00

   Total cost _____

3. List price: $4,025

   Sales tax rate: 5%

   Title fee: $37.50

   License plate fee: $46.30

   Total cost _____

4. List price: $3,695

   Sales tax rate: 6%

   Title fee: $20.75

   License plate fee: $38.00

   Total cost _____

Looks

B Find the sales tax and the total cost of each used car.

	List Price	Sales Tax Rate	Sales Tax	Title Fee	License Plate Fee	Total Cost
5.	$4,000	5%		$17.50	$25.00	
6.	$1,750	4%		16.00	15.00	
7.	$6,500	5%		38.00	18.75	
8.	$4,995	7%		20.00	22.50	
9.	$8,650	6%		18.50	25.00	
10.	$3,775	4%		13.50	20.00	
11.	$2,500	5%		20.00	19.50	
12.	$7,850	4%		37.50	16.50	
13.	$9,500	6%		49.00	25.00	
14.	$1,250	7%		12.50	18.00	
15.	$5,995	4%		15.00	20.50	
16.	$12,600	5%		56.50	32.00	
17.	$7,695	6%		20.00	21.00	

18. Ken Smith buys a compact car listed at $4,500. The state sales tax rate is 5%. The title fee is $8.50, and the license plate fee is $17.50. In addition, the car needs a new muffler, which costs $125.50. What is the total cost of the car? _____

19. Joan Koko buys a sports car listed at $6,250. The state sales tax rate is 6%. The title fee is $7.50, and the license plate fee is $25.00. The car needs $250.00 of repairs before it can meet the state inspection requirements. What is the total cost of the car? _____

20. How much cash does Joan need if she gets a $1,750 trade-in allowance for her old car?

_____

Pete paid 5% sales tax on the purchase of a used van. The amount of the tax was $195. What was the list price of the van?

_____

Financing a Car

Most people who buy a car cannot pay the total cost at the time of purchase. *Financing* a car is similar to buying on the installment plan. A *down payment* is required. It usually consists of a *trade-in* of an old car or a cash payment, or both. The amount left to be paid is made in monthly installment payments. The sum of the down payment and the installed payments is called the *deferred-payment price.*

Example: Nancy Cho is buying a new car. The sticker price is $11,500. Nancy makes a down payment of 20% and is required to make 36 monthly payments of $295.00. What is the amount to be financed? What is the deferred-payment price?

Down Payment = Sticker price x Percent for down payment

= $11,500 x .20

= $2,300

Amount to be financed = Sticker price – Down payment

= $11,500 – $2,300

= $9,200

The amount to be financed is $9,200.00.

Deferred-payment price = Down payment + Total installment payments

= $2,300 + (36 x $295)

= $2,300 + $10,620

= $12,920

The deferred-payment price is $12,920.

A Find the down payment for each car.

1. Compact car

   Sticker price:

   $10,500

   % down: 20%

   _____

2. Mid-size car

   Sticker price:

   $16,500

   % down: 25%

   _____

3. Full-size car

   Sticker price:

   $24,500

   % down: 10%

   _____

UNIT 6 *PURCHASING A CAR* 65

4. Janie Long's new car has a sticker price of $14,500. She makes a down payment of 15%. How much is to be financed? _____

5. Tim West bought a new car with a sticker price of $12,750. He made a down payment of $2,000 and is required to make 48 payments of $268.75. What is the deferred-payment price? _____

B Complete the chart below.

	Sticker Price	Percent Down	Down Payment	Monthly Payments	No. of Payments	Total Payments	Deferred-Payment Price
6.	$8,700	20%		$220.50	36		
7.	9,250	10%		245.60	40		
8.	10,500	15%		285.10	36		
9.	6,900	20%		253.00	24		
10.	12,350	25%		231.55	48		
11.	9,500	10%		273.15	36		
12.	5,750	15%		140.50	40		
13.	11,200	20%		225.00	48		
14.	9,800	18%		256.70	36		
15.	8,500	15%		193.40	40		
16.	10,000	24%		344.40	24		
17.	5,800	10%		190.00	30		
18.	15,600	30%		240.00	48		

Rika's new car has a sticker price of $14,560. She makes a down payment of 20% and agrees to make 36 payments of $342. How much more is the deferred-payment price than the sticker price?

_____

Auto Insurance

In order to drive a car, you are required by law to have automobile insurance. The *insurance policy* you receive may include these coverages:

Liability   Pays the cost of any injury or damage for which you are at fault.

Collision   Pays for damages to your car due to an accident.

Comprehensive   Pays for damages to your car due to fire, theft, vandalism, or acts of nature.

The annual *premium* is the amount you pay each year for the insurance.

Example: Bonnie Hargett is 25 years old. The premium is $185.50 for liability coverage, $240.60 for collision coverage, and $32.75 for comprehensive coverage. What is the annual premium?

$$\boxed{\text{Annual premium}} = \boxed{\begin{array}{c}\text{Cost of}\\\text{liability}\end{array}} + \boxed{\begin{array}{c}\text{Cost of}\\\text{collision}\end{array}} + \boxed{\begin{array}{c}\text{Cost of}\\\text{comprehensive}\end{array}}$$

$$= \ \$185.50 \ + \ \$240.60 \ + \ \$32.75$$
$$= \ \$458.85$$

The annual premium is $458.85.

A Find the annual premium.

1. Sally Feinstein

   Premiums:

   Liability, $175.00

   Collision, $185.00

   Comprehensive, $25.15

   Annual premium _____

2. Jorge Cardenas

   Premiums:

   Liability, $205.10

   Collision, $212.50

   Comprehensive, $40.25

   Annual premium _____

3. Rodney Simpson

   Premiums:

   Liability, $194.00

   Collision, $210.00

   Comprehensive, $28.10

   Annual premium _____

4. Hanna Brown

   Premiums:

   Liability, $220.30

   Collision, $195.40

   Comprehensive, $35.75

   Annual premium _____

Insurance companies use tables such as this one to determine the premiums for liability insurance. Bodily injury limits of 15/30 means that the insurance will pay up to $15,000 to any one person injured and up to $30,000 if more than one person is injured.

Property Damage Limits	Bodily Injury Limits			
	15/30	25/100	50/100	100/300
$10,000	$90.50	$102.00	$105.50	$115.75
25,000	95.65	104.50	112.85	120.15
50,000	99.50	110.75	115.10	125.90
100,000	105.75	120.40	131.65	145.95

B Use the table above to find the cost of liability insurance. Then find the annual premium.

Coverages		Liability	Collision	Annual Comprehensive	Premium
Prop. Dam.	Bodily Injury				
5. $10,000	25/100		$180.75	$40.60	
6. 50,000	25/100		165.90	25.55	
7. 25,000	50/100		175.85	30.15	
8. 10,000	50/100		195.65	18.95	
9. 100,000	50/100		205.15	32.90	
10. 100,000	100/300		197.50	40.75	
11. 50,000	15/30		167.80	34.60	
12. 100,000	25/100		210.65	38.65	
13. 10,000	50/100		165.40	27.60	
14. 25,000	50/100		195.75	41.65	

15. Jake's annual premium is $967.20. He pays $346 for liability coverage and $299.70 for collision coverage. How much does he pay for comprehensive coverage? _____

16. Christine's annual premium is $864.88. She pays her auto insurance in quarterly payments. How much does Christine pay each quarter? _____

 Dennis pays an annual auto insurance premium of $1,250. Twenty percent of the premium is for collision, 35 percent of the premium is for liability, and 45 percent of the premium is for comprehensive coverage. How much does Dennis pay for each coverage?

_____   _____   _____

Depreciation

As a car gets older, its trade-in value decreases. This loss in value is called *depreciation*. The greatest depreciation occurs during the first year. This is an estimated table of depreciation:

First year	30% of original price
Second year	18% of original price
Third year	15% of original price
Fourth year	11% of original price
Fifth year	10% of original price

Example: Jim Robinson bought a new car 3 years ago. He paid $12,500. What is the depreciation after 3 years? What is the estimated value of the car now?

Rate of depreciation = 30% + 18% + 15%

= 63%

Depreciation   = Rate of depreciation x Original price of car

= .63 x $12,500

= $7,875.00

The depreciation is $7,875.00.

Depreciation   = Original price – Depreciation

= $12,500 – $7,875

= $4,625

The estimated value of the car is $4,625.

A Find the amount of depreciation on a car originally priced at $8,000.

1. 1 year   _____

2. 2 years   _____

3. 3 years   _____

4. 4 years   _____

5. 5 years   _____

B A new car costs $12,580. Find the estimated value of the car after the given number of years.

6. 1 year _____

7. 2 years _____

8. 3 years _____

9. 4 years _____

10. 5 years _____

C Find the depreciation and estimated value of each new car. Use the table on page 69 to find the rate of depreciation.

	Type of Car	Original Price	Age of Car	Rate of Depreciation	Depreciation	Estimated Value
11.	Van	$21,000	3 years			
12.	Sports car	25,000	4 years			
13.	Compact	12,500	2 years			
14.	Full-size	22,500	5 years			
15.	Subcompact	9,500	2 years			
16.	Full-size	23,500	1 year			
17.	Sports car	17,500	3 years			
18.	Compact	9,250	4 years			
19.	Van	22,850	5 years			
20.	Subcompact	7,650	1 year			
21.	Compact	11,500	2 years			
22.	Sports car	32,000	4 years			
23.	Full-size	24,600	5 years			
24.	Van	18,900	3 years			
25.	Subcompact	9,000	2 years			

Driving and Maintaining a Car

There are many expenses involved in driving and maintaining a car. Expenses such as gasoline, tires, and repairs are called *variable expenses*. Expenses that remain the same regardless of how much you drive, such as insurance, registration, and depreciation, are called *fixed expenses*. The cost of operating a car is usually expressed in cost per mile. To find the *cost per mile,* divide the annual variable and fixed expenses by the number of miles driven.

Example: Carol Jones drove 10,000 miles last year. Her variable expenses were gasoline, $688; oil, $12; new tires, $100; and repairs and maintenance, $275. The fixed expenses were insurance, $875; license, $50; and depreciation, $2,000. What was the cost per mile for Carol to drive her car?

Variable Expenses		**Fixed Expenses**	
Gasoline	$688.00	Insurance	$875.00
Oil	12.00	License	50.00
Tires	100.00	Depreciation	2,000.00
Repairs	275.00	Total	$2,925.00
Total	$1,075.00		

Cost per mile = (Variable expenses + Fixed expenses) ÷ Miles driven

= ($1,075.00 + $2,925.00) ÷ 10,000

= $4,000 ÷ 10,000

= $.40

The cost per mile to drive the car is $.40.

A Find the cost per mile.

1. Variable expenses: $1,400.50

   Fixed expenses: $2,500.00

   Miles driven: 12,000

   _____

2. Variable expenses: $2,200.10

   Fixed expenses: $1,800.90

   Miles driven: 7,800

   _____

3. Variable expenses: $1,900.00

   Fixed expenses: $2,300.00

   Miles driven: 11,000

   _____

4. Variable expenses: $1,400.00

   Fixed expenses: $2,800.50

   Miles driven: 9,900

   _____

B Find the cost of these variable expenses.

Car parts/Fluids	Price
Air filter $3.97
Alternator...........................54.75
Antifreeze (gallon) 5.75
Headlight 9.50
Oil (quart) 1.19
Oil filter 2.54
Shock absorber 17.65
Spark plug (each)................1.50
Starter 40.65
Transmission fluid (quart)......2.27
Water pump.......................24.95

5. Alternator _____
   Oil filter _____
   8 spark plugs _____
   5 quarts of oil _____
   Total _____

6. Shock absorber _____
   Headlight _____
   3 quarts of
   transmission fluid _____
   Water pump _____
   Total _____

7. Air filter _____
   4 gallons of antifreeze _____
   Shock absorber _____
   4 quarts of oil _____
   Total _____

C Find the cost per mile.

	Annual Variable Expenses	Annual Fixed Expenses	Total Expenses	Miles Driven	Cost per Mile
8.	$850.00	$1,950.00		10,000	
9.	1,175.00	1,825.00		12,000	
10.	965.00	1,535.00		8,000	
11.	1,080.00	920.00		12,500	
12.	765.00	1,085.00		9,250	
13.	1,295.00	1,015.00		10,000	
14.	985.00	975.00		12,000	
15.	1,575.00	925.00		15,000	

Consumer Checkpoint 2

 Solve each problem. Then circle the letter of the correct answer.

1. Wen's monthly income is $2,860. He budgets 20% for rent, 14% for car payment, and 15% for food. How much money does Wen have left for his other expenses?
   a. $2,000   b. $2,458.60   c. $2,811.00   d. $1,458.60

2. Sandy has a monthly net income of $2,460. She saves $196.80 each month. What percent of her net income does Sandy save?
   a. 8%   b. 10%   c. 4%   d. 12%

3. Tim bought a new car for $12,400. He made a 20% down payment and financed the car for 3 years. The finance charges are $890.00. How much are his monthly car payments?
   a. $413.33   b. $300.28   c. $275.56   d. $225.40

4. Mr. Gomez purchased a new car with a sticker price of $11,720. He made a 10% down payment and contracted to make 48 monthly payments of $231.75. What is the deferred-payment price?
   a. $11,951.75   b. $10,548.00   c. $12,296.00   d. $11,124

5. Joe drove 9,000 miles last year. His variable expenses were $940 and his fixed expenses were $1,460.00. What was Joe's cost per mile?
   a. $.16   b. $.27   c. $.10   d. $.22

6. At the end of the year, Pete's Pedal Place had 7 mountain bikes with a unit cost of $325.00 each; 14 bike helmets with a unit cost of $48.25 each; and 4 touring kits with a unit cost of $54.40 each, in stock. What is the value of Pete's inventory?
   a. $3,185.00   b. $31,681.00   c. $427.65   d. $3,168.10

7. Kara spent $720 on gasoline; $160 on tires; $600 on insurance; and $220 on repairs. How much did Kara spend on variable auto expenses?
   a. $1,700   b. $940   c. $880   d. $1,100

8. Tia's opening credit card balance was $394.21. She made a payment of $125.00 and purchases of $44.95, $26.40, and $16.50. The finance charge was $3.00. What is Tia's new balance?
   a. $360.06   b. $607.06   c. $357.06   d. $485.06

9. Kenji bought an $860 home entertainment system. He made a $120 down payment and 9 monthly installment payments of $89. How much finance charge did Kenji pay?
   a. $59   b. $120   c. $61   d. $179

10. Margaret borrowed $2,800 to buy a computer. She repaid the loan in 24 months by making payments of $125 each month. How much was the finance charge?
    a. $1.25   b. $200   c. $52.08   d. $24

Writing Fractions in Lowest Terms

Rules to Remember:

To write a fraction in lowest terms:

➤ Divide the numerator and denominator by a number that will divide each without a remainder.

➤ Repeat this until the numerator and denominator cannot be divided by the same number except 1.

Examples:

Write $\frac{25}{40}$ in lowest terms.

$$\frac{25}{40} = \frac{25 \div 5}{40 \div 5} = \frac{5}{8} \longleftarrow \text{ lowest terms}$$

Write $\frac{24}{60}$ in lowest terms.

$$\frac{24}{60} = \frac{24 \div 3}{60 \div 3} = \frac{8}{20} \longleftarrow \text{ not in lowest terms}$$

$$\frac{8}{20} = \frac{8 \div 4}{20 \div 4} = \frac{2}{5} \longleftarrow \text{ lowest terms}$$

▮ Write these fractions in lowest terms.

1. $\frac{12}{24} =$　　2. $\frac{10}{15} =$　　3. $\frac{8}{12} =$　　4. $\frac{20}{25} =$　　5. $\frac{9}{18} =$

6. $\frac{18}{24} =$　　7. $\frac{4}{16} =$　　8. $\frac{10}{12} =$　　9. $\frac{14}{16} =$　　10. $\frac{6}{8} =$

11. $\frac{15}{25} =$　　12. $\frac{6}{24} =$　　13. $\frac{3}{15} =$　　14. $\frac{9}{12} =$　　15. $\frac{20}{32} =$

16. $\frac{14}{28} =$　　17. $\frac{9}{36} =$　　18. $\frac{36}{50} =$　　19. $\frac{24}{32} =$　　20. $\frac{50}{75} =$

21. $\frac{15}{45} =$　　22. $\frac{21}{36} =$　　23. $\frac{10}{25} =$　　24. $\frac{9}{45} =$　　25. $\frac{18}{21} =$

26. $\frac{12}{48} =$　　27. $\frac{24}{72} =$　　28. $\frac{18}{50} =$　　29. $\frac{72}{90} =$　　30. $\frac{23}{46} =$

Writing Fractions as Percents

Rules to Remember:

To write a fraction as a percent:

➤ Divide the numerator by the denominator. Carry the division to two places or more.

➤ Write a percent for the decimal.

Examples:

Write $\frac{25}{40}$ as a percent.

$\frac{25}{40}$ means 25 ÷ 40

$$\begin{array}{r} .625 = 62.5\% \\ 40\overline{)25.000} \\ \underline{240} \\ 100 \\ \underline{80} \\ 200 \\ \underline{200} \\ 0 \end{array}$$

$\frac{25}{40} = .625 = 62.5\%$

Write $\frac{12}{18}$ as a percent.

$\frac{12}{18}$ means 12 ÷ 18

$$\begin{array}{r} .66 \; \frac{12}{18} = .66\frac{2}{3} = 66\frac{2}{3}\% \\ 18\overline{)12.00} \\ \underline{108} \\ 120 \\ \underline{108} \\ 12 \end{array}$$

$\frac{12}{18} = .66\frac{2}{3} = 66\frac{2}{3}\%$

Write a percent for each fraction.

1. $\frac{1}{2}$ =

2. $\frac{3}{4}$ =

3. $\frac{5}{8}$ =

4. $\frac{2}{3}$ =

5. $\frac{3}{5}$ =

6. $\frac{9}{10}$ =

7. $\frac{1}{20}$ =

8. $\frac{17}{25}$ =

9. $\frac{1}{3}$ =

10. $\frac{7}{8}$ =

11. $\frac{3}{40}$ =

12. $\frac{3}{10}$ =

13. $\frac{19}{20}$ =

14. $\frac{9}{50}$ =

15. $\frac{5}{6}$ =

16. $\frac{3}{8}$ =

17. $\frac{7}{25}$ =

18. $\frac{5}{16}$ =

19. $\frac{1}{8}$ =

20. $\frac{1}{6}$ =

21. $\frac{7}{10}$ =

22. $\frac{25}{75}$ =

23. $\frac{18}{40}$ =

24. $\frac{16}{25}$ =

25. $\frac{35}{50}$ =

UNIT 7 *TAXES* **75**

Most states have a *sales tax* on certain services and items that are purchased. The rate varies from state to state. The amount of sales tax can be computed, or it can be read from a table.

Example:

Tony Demarco purchased a belt priced at $19.95. The sales tax rate in his state is 6%. Find the sales tax using the chart. What is the sales tax when it is computed? What is the total cost of the belt?

6% SALES TAX SCHEDULE					
Transaction	Tax	Transaction	Tax	Transaction	Tax
.01 - .10	.00	8.42 - 8.58	.51	16.92 - 17.08	1.02
.11 - .22	.01	8.59 - 8.74	.52	17.09 - 17.24	1.03
.23 - .39	.02	8.75 8.91	.53	17.25 - 17.41	1.04
.40 - .56	.03	8.92 - 9.08	.54	17.42 - 17.58	1.05
.57 - .73	.04	9.09 - 9.24	.55	17.59 - 17.74	1.06
.74 - .90	.05	9.25 9.41	.56	17.75 - 17.91	1.07
.91 - 1.08	.06	9.42 - 9.58	.57	17.92 - 18.08	1.08
1.09 - 1.24	.07	9.59 9.74	.58	18.09 - 18.24	1.09
1.25 - 1.41	.08	9.75 - 9.91	.59	18.25 - 18.41	1.10
1.42 - 1.58	.09	9.92 - 10.08	.60	18.42 - 18.58	1.11
1.59 - 1.74	.10	10.09 - 10.24	.61	18.59 - 18.74	1.12
1.75 - 1.91	.11	10.25 - 10.41	.62	18.75 - 18.91	1.13
1.92 - 2.08	.12	10.42 - 10.58	.63	18.92 - 19.08	1.14
2.09 - 2.24	.13	10.59 - 10.74	.64	19.09 - 19.24	1.15
2.25 - 2.41	.14	10.75 - 10.91	.65	19.25 - 19.41	1.16
2.42 - 2.58	.15	10.92 - 11.08	.66	19.42 - 19.58	1.17
2.59 - 2.74	.16	11.09 - 11.24	.67	19.59 - 19.74	1.18
2.75 - 2.91	.17	11.25 - 11.41	.68	19.75 - 19.91	1.19
2.92 - 3.08	.18	11.42 - 11.58	.69	19.92 - 20.08	1.20
3.09 - 3.24	.19	11.59 - 11.74	.70	20.09 - 20.24	1.21
3.25 - 3.41	.20	11.75 - 11.91	.71	20.25 - 20.41	1.22
3.42 - 3.58	.21	11.92 - 12.08	.72	20.42 - 20.58	1.23
3.59 - 3.74	.22	12.09 - 12.24	.73	20.59 - 20.74	1.24
3.75 - 3.91	.23	12.25 - 12.41	.74	20.75 - 20.91	1.25
3.92 - 4.08	.24	12.42 - 12.58	.75	20.92 - 21.08	1.26
4.09 - 4.24	.25	12.59 - 12.74	.76	21.09 - 21.24	1.27
4.25 - 4.41	.26	12.75 - 12.91	.77	21.25 - 21.41	1.28
4.42 - 4.58	.27	12.92 - 13.08	.78	21.42 - 21.58	1.29
4.59 - 4.74	.28	13.09 - 13.24	.79	21.59 - 21.74	1.30

In the tax table, $19.95 falls in the bracket $19.92–$20.08, so the tax is $1.20.

Sales tax = Tax rate x Price

= .06 x $19.95

= $1.197 (rounded to next highest cent = $1.20)
Note: Always round up for sales tax.

Total cost = Price + Sales tax

= $19.95 + $1.20

= $21.15

The total cost of the belt is $21.15.

A Use the sales tax table to find the sales tax.

1. $.59 _____   2. $2.45 _____   3. $9.90 _____

4. $18.95 _____   5. $1.50 _____   6. $10.75 _____

B Use the sales tax table to find the sales tax and total cost of each item.

7. Wallet $18.95

   Sales tax _____

   Total cost _____

8. Book $10.95

   Sales tax _____

   Total cost _____

9. Bottle of soda $1.49

   Sales tax _____

   Total cost _____

10. Hat $11.99

   Sales tax _____

   Total cost _____

C Compute the sales tax and total cost of each item.

	Item Purchased	Selling Price	Tax Rate	Sales Tax	Total Cost
11.	Refrigerator	$650.00	5%		
12.	Book	19.95	6%		
13.	Iron	27.50	6%		
14.	Bicycle	125.00	4%		
15.	CD	10.95	4%		
16.	Tires	215.00	5%		
17.	Swimsuit	28.50	7%		
18.	Used car	4,445.00	6%		
19.	Perfume	43.75	6%		
20.	Flashlight	16.80	5%		

Hannah bought 3 magazines for $2.50 each, $17.40 worth of food, and $4.40 worth of cleaning supplies. The state tax rate is $6\frac{3}{4}$% on nonfood items. What is Hannah's total bill?

_____

Real Estate Tax

People who own real estate must pay a tax based on the *assessed value* of the property. The assessed value is the value used for tax purposes. It is usually some percent of the *market value* (the selling price of the property on the open market). The real estate tax is the product of the assessed value and the *tax rate*.

Example: The Yetmans' house has a market value of $85,000.00. It is assessed for 60% of the market value. The tax rate is $4.00 per $100 of assessment. What is their property tax?

Assessed value = Market value x Rate of assessment

= $85,000 x .60

= $51,000

Assessed value in 100's = $51,000 ÷ 100 = 510

Property tax = Assessed value in 100s x Tax rate

= 510 x $4.00

= $2,040

The real estate tax is $2,040.00.

A Tell how many 100s are in each.

1. $4,000 _____

2. $25,000 _____

3. $78,000 _____

4. $65,800 _____

5. $125,000 _____

6. $104,500 _____

7. $90,900 _____

8. $250,000 _____

9. $82,100 _____

10. $15,400 _____

11. $47,000 _____

12. $8,700 _____

13. $225,500 _____

14. $32,900 _____

15. $28,600 _____

16. $74,700 _____

17. $10,900 _____

18. $101,100 _____

B Find the assessed value of each property.

19. Market value: $42,500
    Rate of assessment: 60% _____

20. Market value: $148,500
    Rate of assessment: 45% _____

21. Market value: $165,900
    Rate of assessment: 40% _____

22. Market value: $95,000
    Rate of assessment: 60% _____

C Find the property tax.

23. Assessed value: $214,500
    Tax rate: $5.00/$100 _____

24. Assessed value: $127,600
    Tax rate: $4.75/$100 _____

25. Assessed value: $42,500
    Tax rate: $6.00/$100 _____

26. Assessed value: $72,850
    Tax rate: $5.15/$100 _____

D Find the assessed value and property tax.

	Market Value	Rate of Assess.	Assessed Value	Tax Rate per $100	Property Tax
27.	$12,500	75%		$4.50	
28.	148,000	45%		5.25	
29.	60,000	60%		4.75	
30.	275,000	50%		4.00	
31.	68,500	60%		6.15	
32.	72,800	55%		5.65	
33.	100,000	65%		4.20	
34.	85,000	50%		6.25	
35.	125,000	40%		7.50	
36.	230,000	45%		6.75	
37.	62,000	30%		3.50	
38.	110,000	48%		5.00	

 A homeowner pays a property tax of $3,000 on his home, which is assessed at 50% of its market value. The tax rate is $5/$100. What is the market value of the home?

_____

Federal Income Tax, Part 1

Anyone who has taxes *withheld* from his or her pay receives a *Form W-2* in January. This form states the total earnings and federal and state taxes withheld from the last year. From this, the income tax due is computed.

Example:

Gross Pay

Federal Income Tax Withheld

a Control number	22222	Void ☐	For Official Use Only ▶ OMB No. 1545-0008		
b Employer's identification number 10-000-2			1 Wages, tips, other compensation 15155.34		2 Federal income tax withheld 1756.00
c Employer's name, address, and ZIP code United Lumber Co. 901 Timber Lane Woodville, WA 48486			3 Social Security wages 15155.34		4 Social security tax withheld 1083.60
			5 Medicare wages and tips		6 Medicare tax withheld
			7 Social security tips		8 Allocated tips
d Employee's social security number 234-56-7890			9 Advance EIC payment		10 Dependent care benefits
e Employee's name (first, middle initial, last) David B. Swanson 4232 Plantation Avenue Salem, OR 97301			11 Nonqualified plans		12 Benefits included in box 1
			13 See instrs. for box 13		14 Other

15 Statutory employee ☐	Deceased ☐	Pension plan ☐	Legal rep. ☐	Hshld. emp ☐	Subtotal ☐	Deferred compensation
f Employee's address and ZIP code						

16 State	Employer's state I.D. No.	17 State wages, tips, etc.	18 State income tax	19 Locality name	20 Local wages, tips etc	21 Local income tax
OR	98-768-0	15155.34	564.35			

Cat. No. 10134D

Department of the Treasury—Internal Revenue Service

Form **W-2** Wage and Tax Statement **1996**

For Paperwork Reduction Act Notice, see separate instructions.

Copy A For Social Security Administration

State Income Tax Withheld

Social Security Tax Withheld

A Study the form and answer the questions.

1. How much was David's gross pay? _____

2. How much federal income tax was withheld? _____

3. What was the amount of state income tax withheld? _____

4. How much was withheld for social security tax (F.I.C.A.)? _____

The federal government taxes your income. To find the *taxable income,* first find the *adjusted gross income.* The adjusted gross income is the sum of all wages, dividends, interest, tips, and other income earned during the year.

Example: Steve Hamilton earns $325.00 a week and has a yearly income from his investments of $3,627.80. What is his adjusted gross income for the year?

Yearly wages = Weekly earnings x 52

= $325.00 x 52

= $16,900

Adjusted gross income   = Yearly wages + Investment income

= $16,900 + $3,627.80

= $20,527.80

His adjusted gross income is $20,527.80.

B Find the adjusted gross income for the year.

5. Weekly wage: $275

Investment income: $3,600

_____

6. Weekly wage: $465

Investment income: $2,750

_____

7. Weekly wage: $322

Investment income: $2,800

_____

8. Weekly wage: $237

Investment income: $1,635

_____

9. Monthly income: $2,450

Part-time job: $950

_____

10. Monthly income: $1,875

Investment income: $5,685

_____

11. Monthly income: $2,270

Investment income: $3,990

_____

12. Monthly income: $2,000

Part-time job: $3,750

_____

To find the taxable income, first find the adjusted gross income (see page 81). The second step is to compute the amount for deductions. Deductions are allowed for such items as medical expenses, taxes paid, and contributions. The last step is to find the amount allowed for exemptions. For each exemption, $2,500 is allowed.

$$\boxed{\text{Taxable income}} = \boxed{\substack{\text{Adjusted}\\\text{gross income}}} - \left(\boxed{\text{Deductions}} + \boxed{\substack{\text{Allowance}\\\text{for exemptions}}} \right)$$

Example: John Stone has adjusted gross income of $33,650. His allowable deductions are $4,675, and he claims 3 exemptions. What is his taxable income?

$$\boxed{\text{Taxable income}} = \boxed{\substack{\text{Adjusted}\\\text{gross income}}} - \left(\boxed{\text{Deductions}} + \boxed{\substack{\text{Allowance}\\\text{for exemptions}}} \right)$$

$$= \$33,650 - (\$4,675 + \$7,500) \quad\longleftarrow\quad 3 \times \$2,500$$
$$= \$33,650 - \$12,175$$
$$= \$21,475$$

The taxable income is $21,475.

A Find the taxable income.

1. John Greene

    Adj. gross income: $19,650

    Deductions: $2,845

    No. of exemptions: 1

    _____

2. Mary Drew

    Adj. gross income: $28,675

    Deductions: $4,305

    No. of exemptions: 2

    _____

3. Chuck Blair

    Adj. gross income: $37,500

    Deductions: $8,615

    No. of exemptions: 5

    _____

4. Lloyd Jones

    Adj. gross income: $88,200

    Deductions: $6,745

    No. of exemptions: 4

    _____

B Find the amount allowed for exemptions and taxable income.

	Adjusted Gross Income	Total Deductions	No. of Exemptions	Amount Allowed for Exemptions	Taxable Income
5.	$26,275	$3,826	2		
6.	15,065	2,178	1		
7.	31,640	4,628	3		
8.	42,800	9,725	4		
9.	25,375	1,200	3		
10.	39,900	5,700	5		
11.	14,290	3,175	2		
12.	62,750	10,695	4		
13.	85,000	17,695	6		
14.	38,275	7,500	3		
15.	123,712	15,683	4		

16. Tom West earned $47,565 in wages and had investment income of $3,625.

He has deductions of $4,675 and claims 5 exemptions.

What is his taxable income? _____

17. Anita Robinson earned $32,800 in wages and had investment income of $4,750.

She has deductions of $3,470 and claims 3 exemptions.

What is her taxable income? _____

18. Roberta Klohr has income of $37,650. Her husband earns an additional income of $32,395.

They file a joint return (combined incomes) and claim $6,975 in deductions.

They claim 5 exemptions.

What is their taxable income? _____

Jean Anderson's taxable income is $38,000. Her deductions are 16% of her taxable income. How much are Jean's deductions?

_____

Addition and Subtraction of Fractions

Rules to Remember:

To add or subtract fractions:

➤ Find the least common denominator (L.C.D.).

➤ Use the L.C.D. to write like fractions.

➤ Add or subtract numerators.

➤ Write the sum or difference over the common denominator.

➤ Write the answer in lowest terms.

Examples:

Add: $\frac{3}{4} + \frac{2}{3}$

L.C.D. = 12

$\frac{3}{4} = \frac{9}{12}$ ◄─── $\frac{3}{4} \times \frac{3}{3}$

$+ \frac{2}{3} = \frac{8}{12}$ ◄─── $\frac{2}{3} \times \frac{4}{4}$

$\frac{17}{12} = 1\frac{5}{12}$ lowest terms

Subtract: $\frac{7}{10} - \frac{1}{3}$

L.C.D. = 30

$\frac{7}{10} = \frac{21}{30}$ ◄─── $\frac{7}{10} \times \frac{3}{3}$

$- \frac{1}{3} = \frac{10}{30}$ ◄─── $\frac{1}{3} \times \frac{10}{10}$

$\frac{11}{30}$ lowest terms

A Add. Use the L.C.D. when needed.

1. $\frac{1}{2} + \frac{3}{4} =$ _____

2. $\frac{2}{3} + \frac{1}{3} =$ _____

3. $\frac{5}{8} + \frac{1}{4} =$ _____

4. $\frac{5}{6} + \frac{1}{3} =$ _____

5. $\frac{3}{5} + \frac{1}{2} =$ _____

6. $\frac{7}{10} + \frac{1}{2} =$ _____

B Add. Use the L.C.D. when needed.

7. $\frac{3}{4} + \frac{1}{8} =$ _____

8. $\frac{2}{3} + \frac{5}{6} =$ _____

9. $\frac{3}{4} + \frac{5}{8} =$ _____

10. $\frac{1}{2} + \frac{9}{10} =$ _____

11. $\frac{7}{8} + \frac{3}{4} =$ _____

12. $\frac{2}{3} + \frac{5}{12} =$ _____

13. $\frac{1}{8} + \frac{1}{3} =$ _____

14. $\frac{7}{8} + \frac{7}{10} =$ _____

15. $\frac{2}{3} + \frac{1}{8} =$ _____

C Subtract. Use the L.C.D. when needed.

16. $\frac{1}{2} - \frac{1}{4} =$ _____

17. $\frac{3}{4} - \frac{1}{2} =$ _____

18. $\frac{5}{8} - \frac{1}{2} =$ _____

19. $\frac{7}{8} - \frac{3}{4} =$ _____

20. $\frac{7}{10} - \frac{1}{5} =$ _____

21. $\frac{7}{12} - \frac{1}{2} =$ _____

22. $\frac{1}{2} - \frac{1}{6} =$ _____

23. $\frac{2}{3} - \frac{1}{4} =$ _____

24. $\frac{9}{10} - \frac{3}{5} =$ _____

25. $\frac{11}{12} - \frac{3}{4} =$ _____

26. $\frac{2}{3} - \frac{1}{3} =$ _____

27. $\frac{5}{12} - \frac{1}{4} =$ _____

28. $\frac{5}{16} - \frac{1}{4} =$ _____

29. $\frac{9}{16} - \frac{1}{2} =$ _____

30. $\frac{15}{16} - \frac{3}{4} =$ _____

31. Scott spent $\frac{3}{4}$ of an hour studying mathematics and $\frac{1}{2}$ hour doing his English assignment. How long did he spend on his homework? _____

32. Christa spent $\frac{3}{4}$ of an hour preparing for a French test and $\frac{5}{8}$ of an hour doing her social studies assignment. How much more time did she spend on her French assignment than on social studies? _____

U
N
I
T
8

One popular way of investing money is to purchase a certificate of deposit. Certificates of deposit usually earn interest at a higher rate than a regular savings account. Certificates for amounts such as $500 or $1,000 may be purchased from a bank. The money loaned to the bank must be left on deposit for a specified time, ranging from 90 days to 8 years. Banks use computers or tables to compute the interest earned.

AMOUNT PER $1.00 INVESTED, DAILY COMPOUNDING						
ANNUAL RATE	INTEREST PERIOD					
	3 MONTHS	ONE YEAR	2.5 YEARS	4 YEARS	6 YEARS	8 YEARS
5.75%	1.014278	1.059180	1.154458	1.258577	1.411952	1.584017
6.00%	1.014903	1.061831	1.161820	1.271224	1.433287	1.616011
6.25%	1.015529	1.064489	1.169103	1.283998	1.454945	1.648651
6.50%	1.016155	1.067153	1.176431	1.296900	1.476930	1.681950
6.75%	1.016782	1.069824	1.183806	1.309932	1.499246	1.715921
7.00%	1.017408	1.072501	1.191226	1.323094	1.521900	1.750579
7.25%	1.018036	1.075185	1.198693	1.336389	1.544896	1.785936
7.50%	1.018663	1.077876	1.206207	1.349817	1.568240	1.822006
7.75%	1.019291	1.080573	1.213768	1.363380	1.591936	1.858806
8.00%	1.019920	1.083278	1.221376	1.377079	1.615989	1.896348

Example: Karl Silex bought a certificate of deposit for $2,000. It earned interest at the annual rate of 7.5%. How much interest did he earn after 2.5 years?

| Amount at maturity | = | Original principal | x | Amount per $1.00 |

= $2,000 x 1.206207

= $2,412.41 (rounded to nearest cent)

| Interest | = | Amount at maturity | – | Original investment |

= $2,412.41 – $2,000.00

= $412.41

The interest earned was $412.41.

A Use the table on the opposite page to find the amount at maturity of each certificate of deposit.

1. Principal: $1,000

   Annual rate: 6.75%

   Interest period: 2.5 years

   _____

2. Principal: $2,000

   Annual rate: 7.00%

   Interest period: 4 years

   _____

3. Principal: $10,000

   Annual rate: 8.00%

   Interest period: 6 years

   _____

4. Principal: $3,500

   Annual rate: 7.75%

   Interest period: 8 years

   _____

B Use the table on the opposite page to find the amount at maturity.
Compute the interest earned.

	Principal	Interest Period	Annual Rate	Amount per $1.00	Amount at Maturity	Interest
5.	$500	4 years	6.00%			
6.	1,000	6 years	6.50%			
7.	1,500	3 months	5.75%			
8.	2,000	1 year	8.00%			
9.	5,000	8 years	7.50%			
10.	2,500	2.5 years	6.25%			
11.	1,000	4 years	6.25%			
12.	4,000	3 months	7.75%			
13.	2,000	6 years	7.50%			
14.	1,500	8 years	7.25%			
15.	5,000	2.5 years	8.00%			
16.	6,000	1 year	7.25%			

Another popular method of investing is the purchase of *savings bonds.* They are guaranteed by the federal government. One type of savings bond is the series EE bond. They can be purchased with a *face value* ranging from $50 to $10,000. The cost of the bond is 50% of its face value. The *redemption value* of the bond includes the cost of the bond plus interest for the time the holder has the bond. The redemption value is based on the redemption value of a $50 bond.

Redemption Value of $50 Series EE Savings Bonds	
After	Redemption Value
6 months	$25.50
1 year	26.40
$1\frac{1}{2}$ years	27.22
2 years	28.14
3 years	30.28
4 years	32.92
5 years	36.12
6 years	39.24
7 years	42.68
8 years	46.46
9 years	50.64

Example: Terrence Brown bought a $300 bond and redeemed it 5 years later. What is the redemption value of the bond? How much interest did he earn?

Cost of bond = Face value x 50%

= $300 x .50

= $150

Redemption value	=	Redemption value of $50 bond	x	Number of $50 in face value

= $36.12 x 6 ◄——— $300 ÷ 50 = 6

= $216.72

Redemption = Redemption value – Cost

= $216.72 – $150.00

= $66.72

The interest earned is $66.72.

A Find the cost of each bond.

1. $50 _____
2. $75 _____
3. $200 _____
4. $500 _____
5. $10,000 _____

B Find the redemption value of each bond.

6. Face value: $150
   Time held: 3 years

   _____

7. Face value: $200
   Time held: 7 years

   _____

8. Face value: $500
   Time held: 5 years

   _____

9. Face value: $1,000
   Time held: 6 years

   _____

C Find the redemption value of and interest on each bond.

	Face Value	Cost of EE Bond	Time Held	Redemption Value of $50 Bond	Redemption Value	Interest
10.	$150		2 years			
11.	200		5 years			
12.	100		6 years			
13.	500		4 years			
14.	100		8 years			
15.	1,000		3 years			
16.	5,000		5 years			
17.	50		7 years			
18.	10,000		6 years			

Buying Stocks

Lesson 3

Another way to invest money is to buy *shares of stock.* When you buy shares of stock, you become part owner of the corporation issuing the stock. The amount you pay for the stock depends on the cost per share, the number of shares you buy, and the *stockbroker's commission.* Stock prices are listed daily in the newspapers.

Example: Sandra Banks purchased 100 shares of AMD at $20\frac{3}{4}$ per share. The stockbroker's commission was $22.55. What was the total amount she paid for the stock?

New York Stock Exchange

Name	Div	Pe	Sales	High	Low	Last	Chg.
AMD	—	—	981	21	20	$20\frac{3}{4}$	$-\frac{1}{4}$
Ball	.82	17	210	$43\frac{1}{4}$	43	$43\frac{1}{4}$	—
BaltGE	1.90	10	785	$30\frac{1}{2}$	30	$30\frac{1}{8}$	$+\frac{1}{8}$
BkNYs	1.68	8	491	$41\frac{1}{2}$	$40\frac{3}{4}$	$41\frac{1}{2}$	$+\frac{1}{8}$
Banner	.06	11	31	22	$21\frac{3}{4}$	$21\frac{3}{4}$	$-\frac{1}{4}$
BASIX	.16	—	862	$7\frac{1}{2}$	$7\frac{3}{8}$	$7\frac{3}{8}$	$+\frac{1}{8}$
BMC	—	—	16	8	$7\frac{1}{8}$	8	—
Cenvill	2.20	9	22	$20\frac{1}{2}$	20	$20\frac{1}{4}$	$-\frac{1}{4}$
ChamSp	—	—	285	15	14	$14\frac{3}{4}$	$-\frac{3}{8}$
Oceana	.40	24	898	$44\frac{7}{8}$	44	$44\frac{3}{4}$	$+\frac{7}{8}$
Sport All	1.00	14	875	$32\frac{1}{8}$	31	$31\frac{1}{4}$	$+1$
Unico	.92	17	109	$30\frac{7}{8}$	$30\frac{1}{2}$	$30\frac{1}{2}$	$-\frac{3}{8}$
WW Mining	2.16	6	1923	$39\frac{5}{8}$	39	$39\frac{5}{8}$	$+\frac{3}{8}$

Cost of stock = Number of shares x Cost per share

$$= 100 \times \$20.75 \longleftarrow \frac{3}{4} = .75$$

$$= \$2,075.00$$

Total amount paid = Cost of stock + Broker's commission

$$= \$2,075.00 + \$22.55$$

$$= \$2,097.55$$

The total amount paid for the stock was $2,097.55.

A Find the cost of these shares of stock.

1. Gail Mitchell

   Number of shares: 100

   Cost per share: $27\frac{1}{2}$

   _____

2. Mike Montoya

   Number of shares: 2,000

   Cost per share: $17\frac{3}{4}$

   _____

3. Tom McMillian

   Number of shares: 250

   Cost per share: $36\frac{1}{4}$

   _____

4. Steven Chambers

   Number of shares: 100

   Cost per share: $32\frac{7}{8}$

   _____

B Find the cost and total amount paid for these shares of stock. Use the last price on the chart on the opposite page for the cost per share.

	Name of Stock	Cost per Share	Number of Shares	Cost of Stock	Stockbroker's Commission	Total Amount Paid
5.	Unico		100		$35.75	
6.	BMC		200		50.15	
7.	BaltGE		150		45.20	
8.	Cenvill		400		72.50	
9.	WW Mining		250		60.85	
10.	BASIX		1,000		120.80	
11.	Oceana		600		85.75	
12.	Sport All		500		75.95	
13.	ChamSp		1,000		125.75	
14.	Ball		600		82.50	
15.	Banner		2,000		200.00	

Stock Dividends

People who own stock receive dividends. *Dividends* are the return on your investment. If the corporation makes a profit, you receive a portion of that based on the number of shares you own. To find the *annual rate of return,* compare the dividend received to the cost of the stock.

Example: Tom Foster owns 200 shares of Val Tex. He receives a dividend of $2.62 per share. What is the amount of his annual dividend? If he paid $32.75 per share, what is the rate of return on his investment?

Total annual dividend = No. of shares x Dividend per share

= 200 x $2.62

= $524.00

The total annual dividend is $524.00.

Rate of return = Annual dividend ÷ Cost per share

= $2.62 ÷ $32.75

= .08 = 8%

The annual rate of return is 8%.

A Find the total annual dividend for each investor.

1. Dale Cleveland

Number of shares: 100

Dividend per share: $1.27

_____

2. Frank Fico

Number of shares: 250

Dividend per share: $1.87

_____

3. Jim Causey

Number of shares: 600

Dividend per share: $2.19

_____

4. Christa Jones

Number of shares: 275

Dividend per share: $1.82

_____

B Find the annual rate of return for each investment.

5. ATM
   Cost per share: $47.50
   Annual dividend: $2.85

   _____

6. TM Tech
   Cost per share: $27.60
   Annual dividend: $1.38

   _____

7. T.E. Enterprises
   Cost per share: $18.25
   Annual dividend: $1.46

   _____

8. AP Corp
   Cost per share: $48.80
   Annual dividend: $3.66

   _____

C Find the total annual dividends and the rates of return.

	Name of Stock	Cost per Share	Number of Shares	Dividend per Share	Total Annual Dividend	Rate of Return
9.	Jetron	$12.75	100	$.51		
10.	AR Press	36.25	80	2.90		
11.	Pan Travel	44.20	75	2.21		
12.	BGT Food	30.00	165	2.25		
13.	Nu Way	65.00	200	3.90		
14.	Coastal	125.00	80	12.50		
15.	AMG Inc.	85.50	500	6.84		
16.	XLMkt	43.60	350	1.54		
17.	LoCo	27.10	110	3.05		
18.	NRail	51.80	420	2.68		
19.	BytCom	87.50	185	4.12		
20.	Star Mfg.	38.50	95	1.07		

Consumer Checkpoint 3

 Solve each problem. Then circle the letter of the correct answer.

1. The Buckleys' house has a market value of $210,000. It is assessed at $\frac{1}{4}$ of its market value and the tax rate is $8\frac{1}{4}$%. How much do the Buckleys pay in property tax?
   a. $17,325.00   b. $1,680.00   c. $433.12   d. $4,331.25

2. Jean purchased a jacket for $110, gloves for $16, and a pair of boots for $58. The state tax rate is 4%. What was the total cost of Jean's purchases?
   a. $191.36   b. $184.00   c. $190.00   d. $7.36

3. The Wilsons have an annual income of $44,160. They claim 4 exemptions and file a joint return. What is their taxable income?
   a. $36,160   b. $54,160   c. $34,160   d. $39,160

4. Phil purchased 75 shares of stock for $763.50. How much did he pay per share?
   a. $8.40   b. $10.18   c. $11.18   d. $12.00

5. The Bay City Investors Club purchased 300 shares of QuikGro at $13.86 per share and 50 shares of RTS at $21.00 per share. The club paid a broker's commission of $140.00. What is the total amount the club paid for the stock?
   a. $5,488   b. $4,018   c. $4,158   d. $5,348

6. Clay bought a $500 series EE bond and redeemed it after 4 years for $329.20. How much interest did Clay earn?
   a. $171.00   b. $79.20   c. $329.00   d. $200.00

7. The Safety Ski Company paid a $1.83 annual dividend per share. If an investor owned 250 shares of Safety Ski stock, how much of an annual dividend would he or she receive?
   a. $670.00   b. $457.50   c. $4,575.00   d. $45.75

8. Hope purchased a certificate of deposit for $1,000. The amount at maturity after 3 years was $1,363.38. How much interest was earned?
   a. $363.38   b. $1,090.14   c. $121.17   d. $1,363.38

9. Carrie purchased a CD for $12.99, a roll of film for $2.79, and a pair of sunglasses for $24.00. She wrote a check for $42.17. What was the sales tax rate on her purchases?
   a. 10%   b. 12%   c. 6%   d. 4%

10. Steve received a dividend of $2.12 per share on a stock he bought for $41.40 per share. Kate received a dividend of $1.80 per share on a stock she bought for $26.10 per share. Who got a higher annual rate of return? How much did he or she receive?
    a. Kate 7%   b. Steve 5%   c. Kate 4%   d. Steve 8%

End-of-Book Test

 Solve each problem. Then circle the letter of the correct answer.

1. Oscar earns $2,675.00 per month. His monthly deductions are $424.12. What is Oscar's annual net income?

   a. $32,100.00   b. $22,250.88   c. $ 17,189.44   d. $27,010.56

2. Veronica deposited checks for $172.41, $75.62, and $417.20 into her savings account. She also made a $53.25 cash deposit. What was her total deposit?

   a. $718.48   b. $665.23   c. $611.98   d. $728.48

3. Mr. Choi earns $600 for a 40-hour week. If he earns time and a half for overtime, what is his hourly overtime wage?

   a. $24.00   b. $7.50   c. $22.50   d. $15.00

4. Rosa's annual income is $30,000.00. She pays $5,400 in income taxes. What percentage of her income does she pay in income taxes?

   a. 6%   b. 15%   c. 18%   d. 162%

5. Bob is a salesclerk at a sports store. He worked 20 hours and earned $265.20. His hourly wage is $4.50. How much did Bob earn in commissions?

   a. $60.00   b. $200.00   c. $88.40   d. $175.20

6. Gary purchased a $8,980 boat on the installment plan. He made a 15% down payment and 12 monthly payments of $650.00. How much was the finance charge?

   a. $650   b. $1,347   c. $1,180   d. $167.00

7. Todd earns $740 weekly and has a yearly income from his investments of $12,222. What is his annual adjusted gross income?

   a. $26,258   b. $38,480   c. $21,102   d. $50,702

8. What is the cost of a $2,000 face value EE savings bond?

   a. $1,000   b. $2,000   c. $750   d. $500

9. Kevin O'Dell has an income of $41,200. He claims 4 dependents and has no allowable deductions. What is his taxable income?

   a. $31,200   b. $41,200   c. $33,200   d. $51,200

10. A realtor sold some property for $62,740. Her commission rate is $5\frac{1}{4}$%. How much commission did the realtor earn?

   a. $3,137.00   b. $3,293.85   c. $6,274.00   d. $4,293.85

11. Kiyo has $1,400 in a savings account that pays 5% annually. The interest is compounded quarterly. How much will Kiyo have in her account after 9 months?

    a. $1,405.00   b. $1,543.50   c. $1,453.16   d. $1,470.00

12. The Bakers have a monthly net income of $3,125. They have budgeted 24% of their income for rent. How much can they spend for rent?

    a. $625   b. $750   c. $700   d. $725

13. A customer makes a purchase of $44.85. The state sales tax is $6\frac{3}{4}$%. What is the total amount of the sale?

    a. $43.08   b. $26.91   c. $49.85   d. $47.88

14. During the past four months, the Winslows have spent $212, $196, $214, and $172 on utilities. What is their average expenditure for utilities?

    a. $190.00   b. $208.00   c. $198.50   d. $188.50

15. Barbara purchased a $790 video camera. She made a 15% down payment. How much was the down payment?

    a. $118.50   b. $79.00   c. $11.85   d. $84.50

16. A sports car has a base price of $16,400, options totaling $1,785, and a destination charge of $525. What is the sticker price?

    a. $18,185   b. $18,710   c. $17,660   d. $18,910

17. Jenny pays $300.00 for liability coverage, $193.40 for collision coverage, and $240.00 for comprehensive coverage. What is Jenny's annual premium for auto insurance?

    a. $1,466.80   b. $540.00   c. $733.40   d. $833.40

18. Mr. Herrera purchased a car with a sticker price of $10,430.00. He made a down payment of 20%. How much will Mr. Herrera finance?

    a. $9,086.00   b. $12,516   c. $8,344   d. $8,354

19. Wendy drove 18,000 miles last year. Her variable auto expenses were $2,200, and her fixed expenses were $3,000. What was Wendy's cost per mile?

    a. $.17   b. $.12   c. $.27   d. $.29

20. Dean owns 400 shares of stock that he purchased for $8.32 per share. He receives a dividend of $.80 per share. What is Dean's annual dividend?

    a. $320.00   b. $665.60   c. $332.80   d. $32.00